The Intelligent
Asset Allocator

The Intelligent Asset Allocator

How to Build Your Portfolio to Maximize Returns and Minimize Risk

William J. Bernstein

McGraw-Hill

New York   San Francisco   Washington, D.C.   Auckland   Bogotá
Caracas   Lisbon   London   Madrid   Mexico City   Milan
Montreal   New Delhi   San Juan   Singapore
Sydney   Tokyo   Toronto

Library of Congress Cataloging-in-Publication Data

Bernstein, William J.
 The intelligent asset allocator: how to build your portfolio to maximize returns and minimize risk / by William J. Bernstein.
  p.   cm.
 Includes bibliographical references.
 ISBN 0-07-136236-3
 1. Portfolio management.   2. Asset allocation.   I. Title.

HG4529.5.B47   2000
332.6—dc21   00-042732

McGraw-Hill

A Division of The McGraw·Hill Companies

12 13 14 15   DOC/DOC   0 9 8 7 6

ISBN 0-07-136236-3

Printed and bound by R. R. Donnelley & Sons Company.

McGraw-Hill books are available at special quantity discounts to use as premiums and sales promotions, or for use in corporate training programs. For more information, please write to the Director of Special Sales, Professional Publishing, McGraw-Hill, Two Penn Plaza, New York, NY 10121-2298. Or contact your local bookstore.

 This book is printed on recycled, acid-free paper containing a minimum of 50% recycled, de-inked fiber.

Contents

Preface

On July 31, 1993, I came across an article in *The Wall Street Journal* ("Your Money Matters" series) which examined the performance of various asset allocations for the period 1973–92. The article was based on research done at the T. Rowe Price mutual fund group. The technique used was quite simple: imaginary portfolios were constructed from various combinations of U.S. large and small stocks, foreign stocks, and U.S. bonds, and returns and risks were calculated. The article pointed out that over the 20-year period studied various fixed mixes of the above assets outperformed the single component parts (as well as most professional money managers), with significantly lower risk. I was intrigued. T. Rowe Price kindly sent me the data underlying their calculations, which I analyzed. The results were astonishing—almost any reasonably balanced fixed combination of the four assets outperformed most professional money managers over the same period.

For example, a "simpleton's portfolio" consisting of one quarter each U.S. large stocks, U.S. small stocks, foreign stocks, and U.S. high-quality bonds had a higher return, with much lower risk, than large U.S. stocks alone (represented by the S&P 500 index). The S&P 500, in turn, performed better than 75% of professional money managers over the same period.

I was fascinated by the T. Rowe Price data; here was a simple tool for ascertaining historical asset allocation performance—collect data on the prior performance of various asset classes, and "backtest" returns and risks. To my disappointment, I could find no readily available software which accomplished this; I would have to write my own spreadsheet files. I began to buy, beg, steal or borrow data on a wide variety of assets over several different historical epochs and build portfolio models going back as far as 1926.

The calculations performed by T. Rowe Price and myself contained an important implicit assumption: that the portfolios were "rebalanced" periodically. Rebalancing becomes necessary after a while because some assets in a portfolio will do better than others, and this will alter the original portfolio composition. In order to rebalance the portfolio back to its starting composition, some of the better performing assets must be sold—and the proceeds used to purchase more of the poorly performing assets.

Most experienced investors learn that the key to long-term success lies in a coherent strategy for allocation among broad categories of assets, principally foreign and domestic stocks and bonds. They also understand that market timing and stock or mutual fund picking are nearly impossible long term. They are at best a distraction. Put another way, it is far more important to come up with the right proportion of foreign stocks, U.S. stocks, foreign bonds, and U.S. bonds than it is to pick the "best" stocks or mutual funds or to "call" the tops or bottoms of the markets. (As we shall see later, nobody consistently calls the market, and almost nobody picks stocks or mutual funds with any persistent skill).

If you find this difficult to believe, consider the following: 1987 was not a great year for the U.S. stock market. U.S. large company stocks (represented by the S&P 500) gained only 5.23% that turbulent year, and small company stocks actually lost 9.3%. On the other hand, foreign stocks gained 24.93%. The clumsiest foreign fund manager would have beaten the most skillful small-stock picker that year. In 1992, the opposite would have occurred when U.S. small stocks gained 23.35% and foreign stocks lost 11.85%. Finally, the 1995–1998 period provided unprecedented returns for the biggest U.S. growth stocks but battered almost everything else.

Still not convinced? In the late 1980s, Gary Brinson, a noted money manager and financial analyst, and his colleagues published two sophisticated statistical studies of 82 large pension funds. They concluded that asset allocation accounted for over 90% of the return variability among the funds, with a less-than-10% contribution from market timing and actual stock and bond selection. *In other words, asset allocation policy was 10 times as important as stock picking and market timing combined.* In recent years many observers have suggested that the 90% figure is too high; perhaps asset allocation accounts for only 50% of return variability. Such arguments completely miss the point. Market timing and security selection are obviously important. The only problem is that nobody achieves long-term success in the former, and almost nobody in the latter. *Asset allocation is the only factor affecting your investments that you can actually influence.*

It is thus truly astonishing that so much ink and airtime is wasted on analysts' predictions of the direction of stock or bond prices and on particular stock and mutual fund recommendations. In fact, when Mr. Brinson himself appeared on Louis Rukeyser's *Wall Street Week* in 1994 almost all of his comments were directed toward market timing and almost no attention paid to asset allocation strategy. The gambling instinct is ingrained in human nature, and few can resist speculation on events that cannot be foreseen.

So how do you arrive at the allocation that will provide the most return with the least amount of risk? You can't. But don't feel bad, because neither can anyone else. Not even Mr. Brinson, who until he retired had more assets under management than any other individual on the planet. Sure, you can look at historical data and examine *what has worked in the past,* but don't confuse that with *what will work in the future.* Later we shall look at historical data and attempt to extract from it useful portfolio advice, but the lessons are sparse. First, stocks are riskier than cash. Second, in the future they will probably have higher returns than cash, but not by as much as in the past, particularly the recent past. Third, portfolio diversification reduces risk. And last, index your investments wherever you can.

In fact, if you tire of reading this book and simply want a recipe for a serviceable portfolio, consider the following advice: Purchase the above-mentioned "simpleton's portfolio" consisting of index funds—one quarter each of U.S. large and small stocks, foreign stocks, and a short-term U.S. bond fund. Index funds have become almost as commoditized as computer chips and gasoline, and they are available through most large fund families and "supermarkets." I highly recommend Vanguard. At the end of each year, rebalance your accounts so that each of the four parts are again of equal size. That's it. Setting up the account should take about 15 minutes, and the annual rebalancing should also take about 15 minutes. You can forget about investing for the rest of the year. If the next 20 years are anything like the last 20, then you will outperform the portfolios of 75% of all professional money managers.

In 1996, I placed this book's first edition on-line and began writing regular pieces for my website, Efficient Frontier (http://www.efficientfrontier.com). The reaction to it exceeded my wildest expectations. The hunger of small investors for information about asset allocation and portfolio theory was gratifying, but the response that I received from investment professionals was completely unexpected. Yes, I was told, we all know how important asset allocation is, but its nuts and bolts—the roadmap, if you will—were not at all obvious. The magic of the Internet put me into contact with dozens of folks who shared my fascination with portfolio theory—some well-known, many not. Two more electronic editions followed. These revisions, the dozens of website pieces, and the many discussions about investing and portfolio theory which followed form the basis of this print edition.

Readers will notice several changes from the previous electronic versions. First and foremost, the emphasis on indexing has become even stronger. I've come to the conclusion that active portfolio management is a sucker's game. Although in some areas, like small stocks, REITs (real estate investment trusts), and foreign stocks, active managers appear to be doing well, this outperformance is illusory. I've eliminated most of the sections describing the manual calculation of various portfolio statistics—spreadsheets and financial calculators have made manual techniques obsolete. I suppose that it adds to the understanding of statistical concepts, such as standard deviation, to be able to calculate them by hand, but you'll have to look elsewhere if you want to learn how to do this. I've also adopted a new algorithm for the calculation of rebalanced portfolio returns and happily abandoned the spreadsheet optimization employed in previous versions.

In the past few years, the investment industry has embraced electronic commerce and made a dizzying variety of tools and vehicles available to the investing public. Unfortunately, most of it is so much rope—fund supermarkets, on-line trading, and an enormous volume of securities "research"—with which most investors will hang themselves. But for the prudent investor, benefits abound. The explosion of the Internet has brought a plethora of useful services and made the brightest minds in modern finance available to anybody with a computer, modem, and phone line. Second, and even more important, is the proliferation of inexpensive indexed investment vehicles. Now even the smallest investors can build portfolios as efficiently and almost as cheaply as the biggest players.

Particular thanks go to Jonathan Clements, Robert Barker, Frank Armstrong, John Rekenthaler, David Wilkinson, Steve Dunn, Scott Burns, and the many others who have provided me with advice and countenance over the past few years. I'm deeply grateful to Susan Sharin, whose unique combination of money-management skills and financial knowledge proved invaluable. Finally, the greatest thanks go to my wife, Jane, without whose encouragement and editing support this book would not have been possible.

William J. Bernstein
North Bend, OR

Introduction

Imagine that you are suddenly transported to a country you have never before visited. Trying to find your way home, you are told that there is a new, well-equipped, comfortable, and reliable car parked nearby. You are handed the keys and told to drive to an airport several hundred miles away where a flight home awaits you.

What do you do? Do you stride to the car without further ado, drive away, and hope that by luck you can pick your way to your intended destination? You hesitate. It does not go unnoticed by the locals that you are a rube, and further the proud driver of an expensive automobile. Several sleazy characters crowd around you to offer their expert assistance. Do you trust yourself to one of them?

Hopefully you do neither and instead find the nearest bookshop, purchase a detailed road map, and plot the most efficient route to the airport. Only then do you start on your way.

Most investors find themselves in a very similar situation. Many choose the first course and begin their investing careers with bold action (usually committing a large amount of their capital to a very risky market sector at or near its top). They rarely have a clear idea of exactly where they are headed or how to get there. Many more know that they are lost and depend on the kindness and expertise of strangers (otherwise known as "account executives" or "financial planners") to find their way. All too often, the interests of these "experts" are very different from their clients.

Learning how to invest successfully on your own is much like getting from one city to another in the manner of our fictional traveler. The road map is a simple one and will be briefly described below. The route will pass particular landmarks in a precise order; each one will be described in its own chapter. The journey will be slow and painstaking at times, and there will be no shortcuts. This book cannot be read quickly; it must be methodically consumed, one page and chapter at a time.

The Road Map

1. Take a deep breath, and do nothing for several weeks or months, or as long as it takes to complete the following steps. You are in no rush to immediately and radically alter your finances. You have the rest of your life to get your affairs in order; the time you take learning and planning will be time well-spent.

2. Acquire an appreciation of the nature of and fundamental relationship between risk and reward in the financial markets.

3. Learn about the risk/reward characteristics of various specific investment types.

4. Appreciate that diversified portfolios behave very differently than the individual assets in them, in much the same way that a cake tastes different from shortening, flour, butter, and sugar. This is called *portfolio theory* and is critical to your future success.

5. Estimate how much risk you can tolerate; then learn how to use portfolio theory to construct a portfolio tailored to produce the most return for that amount of risk.

6. At this point you are finally ready to purchase individual stocks, bonds, and mutual funds. If you have succeeded in the above tasks, this is by far the easiest step.

The Intelligent Asset Allocator will take you through the above steps chapter by chapter on your journey to a coherent and effective lifetime investment strategy.

Can you invest successfully without acquiring a solid understanding of risk and reward in the capital markets, and of portfolio theory? Certainly—many people have done so. It is also possible to learn to swim or to fly an airplane without lessons. I don't recommend it.

How to Read This Book

This is not a Grisham novel; the material to be mastered requires some effort. Each chapter forms the foundation for the next, so the book must be read page by page, chapter by chapter; no skipping around allowed. Ideally, the book should be taken with you on vacation and tackled first thing in the morning while you are still fresh. Put it down after an hour or so, and do not pick it up again until the next day.

A facility with numbers will help but is not essential. Some of the key mathematical concepts and techniques are described in greater detail in a few separate "math details" sections. These can be skipped if you have limited time or absence of mathematical interest.

The most important part of this book is Chapter 9, "Investment Resources." Investing is a journey of lifelong learning, and my fondest hope is that this book will instill a thirst for further exploration of the subject.

1

General Considerations

Imagine that you work for your rich but eccentric Uncle Fred. He is a conscientious and kind employer, and after you have spent some years in his service he decides to let you in on the company pension plan. You are 30 years old and will work for your uncle until you retire in 35 years at age 65. Each year he will contribute $5000 to your retirement account. Further, you must pick ahead of time one of two investment choices for the duration of your employment:

Option 1. Certificates of deposit with a 3% annualized rate of return.

Option 2. A most peculiar option: At the end of each year Uncle Fred flips a coin. Heads you receive a 30% investment return for that year, tails a minus 10% (loss) for the year. This option will be referred to as "Uncle Fred's coin toss," or simply, the "coin toss."

The first choice gives you a fixed rate of return and, in fact, an absolutely certain lump sum at the end of your 35 years. You are adept with a financial calculator, and in a few seconds you determine that this option will yield a sum of $302,310 with which to support your golden years. You realize that inflation will diminish the future value of this princely sum. In fact, if inflation is also 3%, you will be left with only $107,436 of current spending power.

The second choice confuses you at first. The thought of losing 10% of your hard-earned retirement money with the toss of a coin is too much to bear. What if you have a string of losing years? If you get tails all 35 years, you could be left with only a pittance for your retirement. On the other hand, if you get heads all 35 years you know that you will bankrupt poor Uncle Fred with your gains—he will owe you $162,000,000!

Let's look a bit more closely at the second choice. Over a long enough period, you will get exactly half heads and half tails. If you represent this with an alternating series of heads and tails, then your return in each two-year period is represented by:

$$1.3 \times .9 = 1.17$$

The first year return of 30% results in your account being multiplied by 1.3, while a 10% loss multiplies your sum by 0.9. For each dollar you had at the beginning of the two-year period, you now have $1.17.

You again get out your calculator and find that a 17% return at the end of two years is the same as an annual return of 8.17%. This is clearly superior to the 3% return of the first option. Of course, you could have a string of bad luck and get tails more than half of the time. However, with some trial and error on your calculator, you discover that you would have to get 12 heads and 23 tails before you come out worse than the first option, and you decide that the odds of this are quite low. You visit your former college statistics professor, who chides you for forgetting that you could have easily calculated the odds of any combination of coin flips with the so-called binomial distribution function. Your blank look elicits a sigh from him, he heads over to his computer, pulls up a spreadsheet program, and after a few keystrokes hands you the graph in Figure 1-1. What are the odds that you will flip less than 13 heads and come out behind? Less than 5%. Actually, this is a bit of an oversimplification. The *order* of the coin tosses matters a great deal. If you toss 16 straight heads then 19 straight tails you will still come out behind, but if you toss 27 straight tails followed by 8 straight heads you will actually come out ahead. However, these are extremely unlikely events, and the preceding formulation and the graph in Figure 1-1 are an accurate representation of the odds in your favor.

The coin toss also introduces the difference between the *average* and the *annualized* return of an asset. Some of you may wonder why

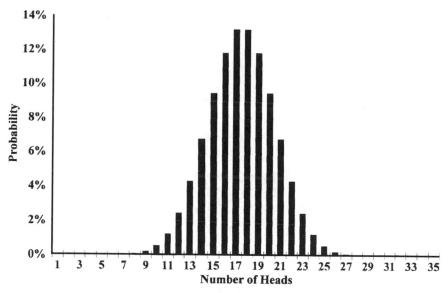

Figure 1-1. Uncle Fred's coin toss probability.

the return of the coin toss is not 10% instead of 8.17%, since the average of +30% and −10% is +10% (30 minus 10, divided by 2). The average return is simply the average of each of the individual annual returns. The annualized return is a more subtle concept. It is the return that you must earn each and every year to equal the result of your series of differing annual returns. If you own a stock which doubles (has a 100% return) the first year and then loses 50% the next year you have a zero annualized return. If the stock was worth $10 per share at the start, it was worth $20 at the end of the first year, and $10 again at the end of the second year. You have made no money, and yet the *average* return is a so-called 25% (the average of +100% and −50%). Your *annualized* return is zero. The annualized and average return clearly are not the same. The coin toss has an average return of 10% and an annualized return of 8.17%. The annualized return is always less than the average return. If in the coin toss you come up with half −10% and half +30% returns, this is the same as having an 8.17% return each and every year. You pay your bills with annualized return, not average return. This is why annualized returns are so important.

Uncle Fred's coin toss may seem a most bizarre scenario, and yet it is nearly identical to the choice faced by most investors between the "safety" of money market accounts or Treasury bills and the "gamble" of common stocks. The second option offers a near certainty of a superior result, yet comes at a price: the small possibility of an inferior result and, more importantly, that gut-wrenching coin toss session with Uncle Fred each year. Yet, it is the 3% certificate of deposit option which is the most truly frightening—you will almost certainly live your golden years in poverty.

I constructed Uncle Fred's coin toss with some deliberation—it's easy to grasp and quite closely approximates the returns and risks of common stocks. The return of common stocks over the past 73 years (1926–1998) was 11.22%, in the same league as the coin toss. More importantly, the "riskiness" of the coin toss and of common stocks are nearly identical. I shall explain shortly how to measure precisely this riskiness. The coin toss is a handy symbolic representation of the risks and returns of common stocks. It will also provide a powerful way in which to understand the behavior of portfolios with multiple asset types.

You have just been introduced to one of the fundamental laws of investing: in the long run you are compensated for bearing risk. Conversely, if you seek safety, your returns will be low. Experienced investors understand that reward and risk are inextricably intertwined; one of the most reliable ways to spot investment fraud is the promise of excessive returns with low risk.

Let's consider an example of investment return slightly more complex than the coin toss. Say that you have invested in asset A (it doesn't matter what it is). The returns for eight consecutive years are as follows:

Year 1:   20%

Year 2:   0%

Year 3:   10%

Year 4:   −10%

Year 5:   30%

Year 6:   15%

Year 7:   10%

Year 8:   5%

What is your return on asset A? In year 1 your return was 20%, so you multiply your asset value by 1.2. In year 2 you multiply by 1.0. In year 3 you multiply by 1.1, and in year 4, when you lose 10%, you multiply by 0.9. Thus, over the full eight years your final value is calculated as:

$$1.2 \times 1.0 \times 1.1 \times 0.9 \times 1.3 \times 1.15 \times 1.1 \times 1.05 = 2.051$$

In this example, if asset A was worth $10 at the beginning of the period, it is now worth 2.051 times the original value, $20.51. The total return over eight years is 105.1%. (Don't be confused by this; remember that a gain of 50% means multiplying your initial amount by 1.5, and that a gain of 100% means multiplying by 2.) The average return is simply the average of the eight individual returns, or 10%. However, we know that what really counts is the *annualized* return (that is, the return which would be required each year to yield the same result). How do we calculate this? If you are familiar with spreadsheets this is a snap—all spreadsheet packages have extensive financial calculation capability. If you are unfamiliar with spreadsheets, then the easiest way to do this is with a financial calculator. If you do not own one, you should. The Texas Instrument BA-35, or its equivalent, can be found in almost any large drug or general merchandise store. It should cost about $20. I urge you to learn how to use the annuity features on this or a similar device—you will find it indispensable for planning your retirement, calculating loan payments, etc. This calculator also has a statistical function that will enable you to rapidly calculate investment risk from a series of returns. Plugging the numbers into the annuity function, we find that the annualized return for the above example is 9.397%. It should not surprise you that this is slightly less than the 10% average return, since annualized return is always less than average return.

The Standard Deviation

We are now ready to calculate the risk of asset A. This is done by calculating a *standard deviation,* or SD, which is a measure of the "scatter" of a set of numbers. Its calculation can be done by hand, but this is quite tedious. Again, this is typically done with a spreadsheet or financial calculator. In the case of the above eight returns, the SD was 11.46%.

What do you do with a standard deviation? First and foremost, you should become familiar with this as a measure of risk. Typically, the standard deviation of the annual returns for various asset classes are as follows:

Money market (cash): 2%–3%

Short-term bond: 3%–5%

Long-term bond: 6%–8%

Domestic stocks (conservative): 10%–14%

Domestic stocks (aggressive): 15%–25%

Foreign stocks: 15%–25%

Emerging markets stocks: 25%–35%

Almost all of the mutual fund rating services list the SD in their reports. Morningstar Inc., a company that compiles information about and analyzes mutual funds, lists standard deviations of annual returns for the preceding 3, 5, and 10 years. In some cases you may have returns for only a year or two. Here the standard deviation of annual returns may be estimated by multiplying the quarterly return SD by 2 or the monthly return SD by 3.46. *Anytime a salesperson or broker attempts to sell you a security of any type, ask him or her what its standard deviation of annual returns is (or is expected to be if it is a new offering).* If he or she doesn't know, don't even think about buying it. If your broker is not familiar with the concept of the standard deviation of returns, get a new one.

What does the standard deviation number actually mean? It means that two-thirds of the time the annual return of the asset will lie between 1 standard deviation above and 1 standard deviation below the mean value. In the case of asset A this means that two-thirds of the time it will be between −1.46% (10 minus 11.46) and 21.46% (10 plus 11.46). I've graphed the "downside" for asset A in Figure 1-2. This shows that there is a 1-in-6 chance of a loss worse than 1.46%. There is a 1-in-44 chance of a loss worse than 12.92% (2 standard deviations less than the mean) and a 1-in-740 chance of a loss worse than 24.38% (3 standard deviations below the mean). To use a simpler example, let's assume that you are considering a Latin

Math Details: Other Measures of Risk

Those of you with sophisticated math backgrounds will recognize the limitations of the SD as a measure of risk. For example, in the real world of investing, returns do not follow a classic "normal distribution," but instead more closely approximate a lognormal distribution. Further, there is a degree of asymmetry about the mean (skew) as well as a somewhat higher frequency of events at the extremes of range (kurtosis). The most important criticism of standard deviation as a measure of risk is that it assigns equal importance to returns both above and below the mean, whereas clearly only events occurring below the mean are of importance to any measurement of investment risk. This has prompted some academics and practitioners to suggest "semivariance," or the mean variance of events occurring below the mean, as a more realistic measurement of risk. In practice, however, both variance and semivariance yield very similar results, and variance/standard deviation is still an excellent measure of risk. In fact, simple variance/SD has the additional advantage of giving you two chances of catching excessive volatility. In the recent notorious case of Long Term Capital Management, the firm did not develop a significantly negative semivariance until shortly before bankruptcy. Simple calculation of the plain-vanilla SD/variance of monthly returns would have warned of trouble years before the ottoman hit the fan.

There are nearly as many definitions of risk as there are finance academics. Other possible measures include the probability of a nominal loss, or an inflation-adjusted loss, a "loss standard deviation," or the probability of underperforming a given index, such as the S&P 500 or T-bill yield. A measure favored by many is the probability that your investment will underperform a risk-free asset, usually T-bills. This is easily calculated from a formula using a "standard normal cumulative distribution function," similar to the binomial distribution function used by our hypothetical statistics professor.

You can easily make up your own risk measure. Such individual measures of risk and return are referred to as *utility functions*.

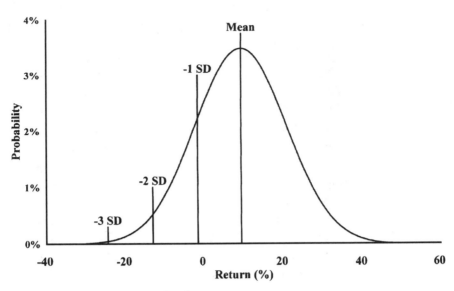

Figure 1-2. Asset A returns distribution.

American stock fund with an expected return of 15 and a very high SD of 35%. This tells you to expect a loss of 20% or worse every 6 years, a loss of worse than 55% every 44 years, and a loss of 90% every 740 years. I very much doubt that many of the fund salespeople or brokers touting these funds in recent years conveyed such information to their clients. In fact, one sign of a dangerously overbought market is a generalized underappreciation of the risks inherent in it.

If you have digested all of the material in this chapter thus far, you have either worked very hard or you are good with numbers (or you have had a course in statistics). Take the rest of the day off, sit by the pool, have a margarita. You've earned it. When you return, we shall begin our consideration of real assets.

2

Risk and Return

Individual Asset Classes: 1926–1998

You should now have a grasp of the statistical meaning of return and risk. You are ready to tackle the long-term historical record of a wide range of assets. Presumably, you would not purchase a car or refrigerator without checking its performance and repair record in a suitable publication like *Consumer Reports.* In a similar fashion, you should not commit a sizable portion of your disposable income to an investment without a good idea of its expected return (performance) and risk (repair record). Fortunately, there is a large amount of useful data out there waiting for you, and it is easily accessible and cheap. How long does it take to get a good idea of the long-term return and risk of an asset class? Opinions vary, but at least 20 or 30 years of data are necessary to get a good idea of expected return. You can get a good idea of asset risk by looking at monthly data for not much more than 5 or 10 years.

When it comes to U.S. securities, we are sitting in clover; there is usable data going back to the birth of the Republic regarding common stocks and government bonds, and extremely detailed data going back to 1926. One of the great bargains in the investing world is the Ibbotson monograph, *Stocks, Bonds, Bills, and Inflation* (known in the investing world as "the SBBI"). This contains every possible breakdown for returns, risks, and correlations of a large

Table 2-1. Asset Classes from 1926 to 1998

Asset	Annualized return, 1926–1998 (%)	Standard deviation, 1926–1998 (%)	Worst return for a single year, 1926–1998 (%)	Return for 1929–1932 (%)
30-day T-bills	3.77	3.22	0.00	+9.49
5-year Treasuries	5.31	5.71	−5.13	+20.27
20-year Treasuries	5.34	9.21	−9.19	+19.73
Large stocks	11.22	20.26	−43.35	−64.23
Small stocks	12.18	38.09	−59.12	−87.98

number of U.S. assets for periods ranging from a month to decades. We shall consider five assets: large and small U.S. stocks, and 30-day, 5-year, and 20-year Treasury securities. Table 2-1 summarizes what you really need to know about U.S. stocks and bonds in the aggregate—it would not be a bad idea to commit the approximate return and SD figures for these five assets to memory.

Let's review each asset individually. You should refer to the accompanying series of graphs for each asset. The terminology for government securities is confusing. A security of less than 1 year is called a Treasury bill, or more simply, a T-bill. An obligation of 1 to 10 years is called a note, and of greater than 10 years a bond.

Treasury Bills.   A Treasury bill (see Figure 2-1) is the safest investment on earth. Short of national destruction, there is no possibility of default, although Uncle Sam occasionally prints money to make good. The price paid for this safety is steep; the return is only 3.77%, which is barely above the inflation rate of 3.08% for the 1926–1998 period. Further, although many academicians consider T-bills to be "riskless," a quick perusal of the T-bill graph shows considerable variation of return, meaning that you cannot depend on a constant income stream. This risk is properly reflected in the SD of 3.22%. The best that can be said for the performance of T-bills is that they keep pace with inflation *in the long run,* although there were prolonged periods when even this was not true, particularly in the 1970s.

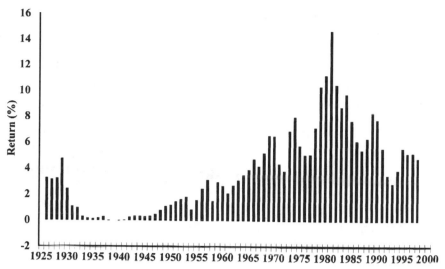

Figure 2-1. Treasury bills, 1926–1998.

Intermediate-Term (5-Year) Treasury Notes. Like T bills, intermediate-term (5-year) Treasury notes (see Figure 2-2) offer near absolute protection from default on principal and interest, but do carry one risk—that of rising interest rates. A note or bond yielding a fixed coupon will decline in market value when interest rates rise, and the longer the maturity of the note or bond the worse the damage. At a maturity of five years, the loss in principal market value can exceed the coupon of the note or bond, resulting in a negative total return for the year This has happened seven times in the past 73 years, and, in fact, the worst loss for this period (2.65%) occurred in 1994. For bearing this risk, you are rewarded with another 1.5% of long-term return. In the long run, the real (inflation-adjusted) return was about 2%.

Long-Term (20-Year) Treasury Bonds. Long-term Treasuries behave in much the same way as the intermediate notes, except that their interest rate risk is much worse, producing losses in 20 of the past 73 years, with one loss of nearly 10%, and many losses in excess of 5% (see Figure 2-3) Surprisingly, you do not seem to be rewarded at all for bearing this risk; the return is almost identical to that of five-year notes.

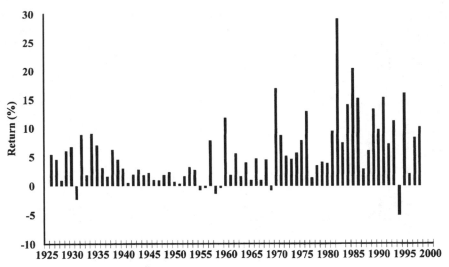

Figure 2-2. Five-year Treasury note, 1926–1998.

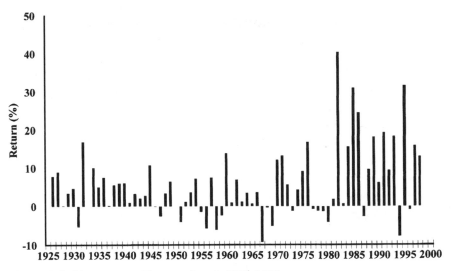

Figure 2-3. Twenty-year Treasury bond, 1926–1998.

Why do many sophisticated investors invest in long bonds when they can have the same return with less risk with intermediate bonds? The answer, which we shall explore in later chapters, is that much of the "excess risk" of long Treasuries disappears in a properly constructed portfolio. That part of the risk that disappears with diversification is called *nonsystematic risk,* and that part which remains and cannot be diversified away is called *systematic risk.* There is another reason why the returns on long Treasuries (and other long bonds) are so low: They are a favorite investment of insurance companies, which have long-lived fixed liability commitments that can be precisely offset with long bonds.

In fact, there are many assets whose apparent risks seem out of proportion to their meager returns. The best example of this is the class of precious metals stocks, with real long-term returns of a few percent and an annual SD of about 30%.

Large Company Common Stocks. For the past 73 years, this asset class has consisted of various groups of large companies, or "indexes." The latest incarnation is the familiar S&P 500. The reader may find the terminology of this group confusing. They are referred to variously as "large stocks," "the S&P," or "the S&P 500." For the purposes of this book, all of these terms are interchangeable.

The rewards of this asset are considerable: a real return of greater than 8% (see Figure 2-4). The lure of common stocks is undeniable your inflation-adjusted wealth will double every nine years. Put away $10,000 for your newborn child, and in 50 years he or she will have $470,000 of current spending power for your grandkids' college educations. This return does not come free, of course. The risks can be stomach-turning. The SD for large company common stocks is 20.26%. (This is the number behind Uncle Fred's coin toss—its SD is also 20%.) You can lose more than 40% in a bad year, and during the four calendar years 1929–1932 the inflation-adjusted ("real") value of this investment class decreased by almost two-thirds!

Small Company Stocks. Companies whose total outstanding stock value, or "market cap," places them in the bottom 20% of the New York Stock Exchange by size are considered small company stocks. (In the current era most of these stocks are actually traded over the counter.) Here, the returns and risks are industrial grade (see Figure 2-5). Your real return is now greater than 9%, meaning that you will double your money in inflation-adjusted terms in just eight years. Put away $10,000 for your grandkids and you will have $785,000 in 50 years in current spending power. But oh, the risks: for 1929–1932 this investment class lost over 85%!

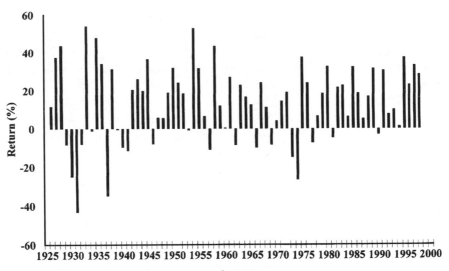

Figure 2-4. Common stock returns, 1926–1998.

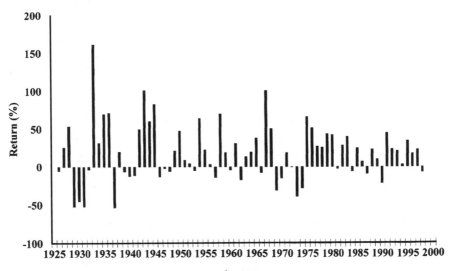

Figure 2-5. Small stock returns, 1926–1998.

Figures 2-6 and 2-7 show the effects of longer holding periods for large company U.S. stocks. Figure 2-6 shows rolling five-year returns for large stocks; except for the Great Depression, things do not look so scary, with only a few losing periods. The picture shown in Figure 2-7 for 30-year holding periods is positively tranquil; there is not a

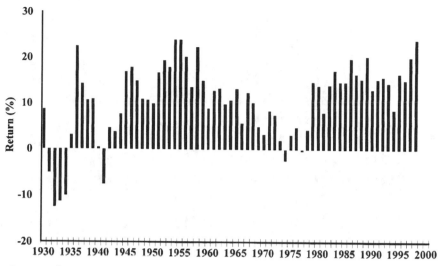

Figure 2-6. Common stock 5-year returns, 1926–1998.

single 30-year period with a return of less than 8%! The message is clear: stocks are to be held for the long term. Don't worry too much about the short-term volatility of the markets; in the long run, stocks will almost always have higher returns than bonds.

This subject can also be analyzed from a theoretical viewpoint. Using some relatively simple statistical methods, you can calculate the risk of underperforming the "risk-free" T-bill investment. This method assumes a return on common stock of 10%, an SD of 20%, and a T-bill rate of 3%. In any given year, the risk of stocks underperforming T-bills is 36%. For a 5-year period, this risk is 22%; for 10 years, 13%; for 20 years, 6%; for 30 years, 3%; and for 40 years, it is only 1%. The message is the same: the longer one's time horizon, the less likely the risk of loss.

A word of caution here. Some have interpreted the above data as demonstrating that stocks grow less risky with time. This is not quite true. Take a look at Figure 2-7. The difference between the highest and lowest 30-year return is almost 5%. Compounding a 5% return difference over 30 years produces an almost fourfold difference in end wealth. Figure 2-8 demonstrates the vastly different end wealth of $1 invested over the various 30-year periods since 1926. This graph shows that when you measure risk as the standard deviation of end

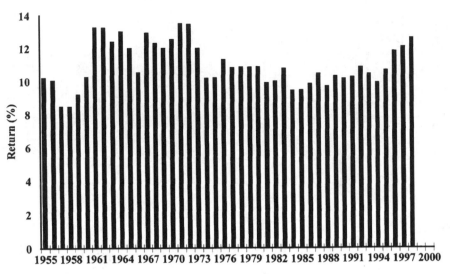

Figure 2-7. Common stock 30-year returns, 1926–1998.

wealth, stocks actually become *riskier* with time. This is not a trivial or theoretical distinction. Probably the most relevant definition of risk is the likelihood of running out of money. It is vitally important that you think about what measure of risk best describes your own personal needs and perceptions.

Everybody's Grandchildren Ought to Be Rich

In the halcyon early summer of 1929, John J. Raskob, a senior financier at General Motors, granted an interview to *The Ladies Home Journal*. The financial zeitgeist of the late 1920s is engagingly reflected in a quote from this piece:

> Suppose a man marries at the age of twenty-three and begins a regular savings of fifteen dollars a month—and almost anyone who is employed can do that if he tries. If he invests in good common stocks and allows the dividends and rights to accumulate, he will at the end of twenty years have at least eighty thousand dollars and an income from investments of around four hundred dollars a month. He will be rich. And because anyone can do that I am firm in my belief than anyone not only can be rich but ought to be rich.

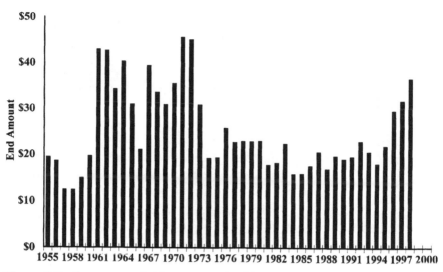

Figure 2-8. Common stock 30-year growth of $1.

Mr. Raskob's hypothetical young man was an investment genius indeed—turning $15 per month into $80,000 in 20 years requires an annualized rate of return of over 25%. This interview and the investment scheme he was promoting are remembered to this day as an absurd example of the infectious mood underlying the pre-1929 stock bubble.

And yet, in the long run, Mr. Raskob was not far off the mark. Let's imagine that Mr. Raskob's hypothetical young man began investing $15 per month in common stocks on January 1, 1926 and continued doing so until he died at age 91 on December 31, 1994. By that date he would have accumulated $2,462,295. Had he invested in small stocks, he would have $11,730,165. Obviously, this calculation contains a number of unrealistic assumptions: that the principal and dividends were never spent, taxes were not paid, and stocks were bought free of commissions. Perhaps our estimates are off by a factor of 2 or 3; still, the long-term results are impressive. An optimist might cite this as an example of the "magic of compound interest." Too much is made of this phenomenon. A pessimist would note that our industrious saver died an old man without enjoying his fortune. Had he consumed even a small percentage of his savings each year, his estate would have been vastly smaller. Personally, I'd rather be a

26-year-old roaming the boulevards of Paris with a few francs in my pocket than a rich old man. Everyone cannot be rich, but perhaps their grandchildren can.

I urge you to spend a few minutes perusing Figures 2-1 to 2-8 so that you are suitably impressed with the magnitude of the risks involved in bonds and common stocks. The next 73 years will likely be just as bumpy as the last.

Individual investors are inevitably drawn into stocks during powerful bull markets; the spectacle of one's friends and neighbors achieving quick and effortless profit awakens the powerful forces of human nature. Those sucked into the market for the first time during such enthusiasms invariably lack a proper appreciation of the risks associated with high returns; they draw comfort from the blandishments of experts that they can "keep close to the exits" and sell their stocks the moment the bear growls. After they have suffered the inevitable losses, they are overcome by an even more powerful element of human financial nature: the urge to psychologically distance themselves from their "failure," and thus sell at a great loss, usually when prices are the lowest. The plain fact of the matter is that no investor, no matter how skilled, ever avoids bone-crushing losses at times, even when undertaking the most prudent market risks. All investors, novice or experienced, are well served by the words of John Maynard Keynes:

> I do not feel that selling at very low prices is a remedy for having failed to sell at high ones. . . . I feel no shame at being found owning a share when the bottom of the market comes. I do not think it is the business, far less the duty, of an institutional or any other serious investor to be constantly considering whether he should cut and run on a failing market, or feel himself to blame if shares depreciate on his hands. I would go much further than that. *I would say that it is from time to time the duty of the serious investor to accept the depreciation of his holdings with equanimity and without reproaching himself* [italics added]. An investor is aiming, or should be aiming, primarily at long period results, and should be solely judged by these. The fact of holding shares which have fallen in a general decline of the market proves nothing and should not be a subject of reproach.

Fortunately, there are ways to lessen the raw risks of single assets, and there are even times when the addition of a small amount of a very risky asset to your portfolio will actually lessen its volatility.

Asset Classes in the 1970–1998 Period

The previously discussed 1926–1998 database for U.S. assets provides a reliable estimate of the expected long-term return and risk in U.S. stocks and bonds. In fact, there are data on the long-term returns and risks of these assets going back 200 years, albeit considerably less detailed and accurate; the inflation-adjusted returns and SD data are very similar to the 1926–1998 data. (For an excellent discussion of stock returns throughout the entire 200 years of U.S. history, see Jeremy Siegel's *Stocks for the Long Run.*)

Unfortunately, the 1926–1998 database is confined to U.S. equities and high-quality bonds and is thus much too limited to be of real use to the modern investor, who has available a much wider variety of capital markets to choose from. There is great advantage to be gained from wide diversification among as many potential investment categories as possible. All investors, small and large, require accurate estimates of the returns and risks of each of these investments. I have chosen 1970 as the starting point for this expanded database because high quality data are available from this date for a wide variety of assets and because 1970 forms an important watershed in investment history. The bear market of 1973–1974 was the worst down market experienced by the capital markets globally since the Great Depression. It is instructive to include the performance for these two years for each asset as a guide to their risk. Including such a ferocious bear market provides a healthy dose of "reality testing." This database also has one further advantage—it is almost completely accessible from a wide variety of sources, such as Morningstar, for a nominal fee (see Chapter 9 for further details). The returns and SDs for these assets are summarized in Table 2-2.

You have already encountered T-bills, 5-year Treasury notes, 20-year Treasury bonds, the S&P stocks, and small U.S. stocks in the 1926–1998 database. Real estate investment trusts (REITs) are companies that derive their revenue from the management of commercial property. I exclude those REITs that derive their income primarily from mortgage activity, and include only so-called equity REITs. The European, Pacific Rim, and Japanese stock indexes derive from the Morgan Stanley Capital Indexes and represent the largest stocks in those markets. Precious metals stocks represent the gold

Table 2-2. Asset Performance from 1970 to 1998

Asset	Return (%)	Risk (SD) (%)	Worst year (%)	1973–1974 (%)
T-bills	6.76	2.61	+3.00	+15.48
5-year Treasuries	9.03	6.62	−3.58	+10.56
20-year Treasuries	9.66	11.58	−7.78	+3.20
S&P stocks	13.47	15.94	−26.47	−37.25
REITs	13*	17*	−21.40	−33.58
U.S. small stocks	13.62	22.58	−38.90	−56.44
European stocks	13.63	20.30	−22.77	−28.74
Pacific Rim stocks	9.69	31.23	−50.59	−54.80
Japanese stocks	12.61	33.49	−36.18	−27.65
Precious metals stocks	10*	43*	−41.51	+112.83
International small stocks	16.98	31.22	−28.61	−38.38

*Author's best estimates (see text explanation).

SOURCES: Ibbotson Associates, NAREIT, Morgan Stanley Capital Indexes, Dimensional Fund Advisors.

and silver mining industry. Finally, international small stocks are foreign equivalent of U.S. small stocks. This index is kept by Dimensional Fund Advisors, and care is urged in its use because before 1988 it consisted of only two countries: the United Kingdom and Japan.

Casual perusal suggests that returns for the 1970–1998 period are higher than for the 1926–1998 period (about 4% higher for the three bond categories, 1.5% for small stocks, and 2.5% for large stocks). However, inflation for the recent period was 5.23% annualized versus 3.1% for the 1926–1998 period, so real returns were about the same for large stocks, smaller for small stocks, and higher for all the bond categories. Comparing the tables for the two periods also suggests that the 1929–1932 bear market was much worse than the 1973–1974 market. Again, this is largely illusion, as the 1929–1932 bear market was characterized by severe deflation, and the 1973–1974 market by severe inflation. In real terms, the 1929–1932 market was only slightly worse than the more recent one for large stocks.

As with the 1926–1998 database, there is a good correlation between risk and return with two notable exceptions—precious metals stocks and Pacific Rim stocks, whose returns were not commensurate with their risks. Note that data for the returns of both REIT and precious metals stocks are not easily available. To estimate the long-term returns for precious metals stocks, I used the Morningstar mutual fund objective data, which go back to 1976. For the years 1970–1975, I used the returns of a "proxy" mutual fund—the Van Eck Gold Fund. For REITs, I used data from the National Association of Real Estate Investment Trusts (NAREIT), which extends back only to 1971. The makeup of the REIT sector has undergone dramatic changes in the past five years, and the historical NAREIT returns may no longer be representative. *The long-term returns data for REITs and precious metals are highly suspect, and should not be used for planning purposes.* However, even if the returns of these two assets were very low, many investors may still want exposure to them. The main reason for this is that they are perceived to be inflation hedges, and likely to do well in an inflationary environment in which other stocks and bonds would be adversely affected. This is the same as saying that much of the risk of precious metals and REITs can be "diversified away." More about this later in Chapters 3 and 4. Figures 2-9 and 2-10 plot return and risk for the 1926–1998 and 1970–1998 asset bases. The risk for each asset, quantified as the SD, is plotted along the horizontal axis (or x axis). Safe assets are clustered on the left side of the graph; as we move off to the right, risk (SD) increases. Annualized return is plotted along the vertical axis (or y axis). As we move from bottom to top, return increases. Note how for almost all assets, as return increases, so does risk. If we were to draw an imaginary line through the points, it would slope up to the right. Most assets lie on a fairly straight line, showing clearly the direct relationship between risk and return. The two major exceptions to this are precious metals and Pacific Rim stocks, as noted above.

The Problem with Historical Returns

One area which gives even finance professionals real problems is the estimation of future asset returns. One expedient is simply to use

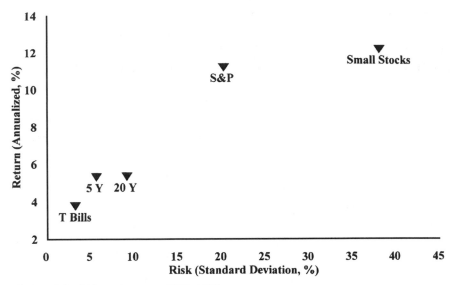

Figure 2-9. Risk and return, 1926–1998.

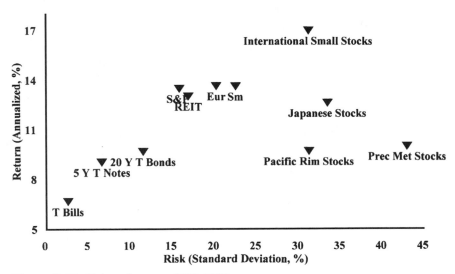

Figure 2-10. Risk and return, 1970–1998.

historical returns; the quality and detail of the available data, particularly from Ibbotson, make this particularly attractive. Most analysts learn from hard experience, however, that it can be hazardous to blindly extrapolate past returns into the future. It is extremely helpful to have an intuitive idea of how to estimate the future returns of stocks and bonds.

Long bonds are relatively easy. A good approximation of their return is simply the coupon. Say you have a 6% 30-year Treasury bond. If interest rates do not change, you will in fact receive a 6% long-term return. If rates fall, then you will obtain a slightly lower return, as the coupons will be invested at a lower rate (so-called reinvestment risk). If rates rise, the opposite will occur. Still, even with significant long-term bond market volatility the long-term return will not be more than a few percent off the coupon rate. At the beginning of 1926, the coupon on long-term AAA corporate bonds was 4.9%—not too far off the actual return for 1926–1998 of 5.77%.

Long bonds also nicely illustrate the dangers of relying on historical returns too heavily. From 1958 through 1983, bonds underwent a brutal, grinding bear market, as long-term Treasury rates rose from less than 3% to over 14%. (Bond prices move in the direction opposite interest rate changes.) Because of this, the annualized return of 20-year Treasury bonds for the 50-year period from 1934 to 1983 was only 3.5%, which was actually slightly less than inflation. Had you relied on this historical return, you would have come up with a ridiculously pessimistic estimate of future bond returns in 1984. As it turns out, in 1984 the 14% coupon for the 20-year Treasury bond more accurately forecasted the 12.85% return over the subsequent 15 years. (The lower annualized return resulting from the fact that the coupons had to be reinvested at an ever-falling rate.) As this book is being written, long Treasuries are again yielding a reasonable 6%, so their expected return should be close to the historical 5% norm.

Stock returns are less easy. Probably the most time-honored method of estimating future stock returns involves the so-called discounted dividend method. It goes something like this: over a long enough time period, all companies go bankrupt. If you don't believe this go to a large reference library and examine a stock page from the Civil War; you'll find that almost none of the names are recognizable. *The value of a stock thus comprises the "discounted value" of all of its future dividends.* (We'll discuss in Chapter 7 just how to go about doing this sort of calculation and precisely what we mean by "discounted value.") If you were a Rip Van Winkle investor who placed $10,000 in the stock market and then went to sleep for 200 years, all you would be left with when you awoke would be generations of reinvested dividends from a long list of mostly defunct companies. (Mind you, this would be a very large amount of money.) Estimating the value of a stock or stock market by this method is a very complicated calculation, but can be simplified as follows:

Return = dividend yield + dividend growth rate + multiple change

Since 1926, stocks actually yielded an average of about 4.5%. Earnings and dividends have grown at about a 5% rate. The term *multiple change* refers to the increase or decrease in the overall dividend rate. In this case, it refers to the fact that stocks which sold for 22 times dividends (a 4.5% rate) in 1926 now sell for 77 times dividends (a 1.3% rate). This calculates out to an annualized multiple change since then of about 1.7%. Add these three numbers together and you get 11.2% compared to the actual historical return of 11.22%. Not too shabby. (There were, of course, a few bumps on the road to that return.)

Unfortunately, as we start the millennium, things look a little different. The current dividend yield of the S&P 500 is about 1.3%. Dividend growth is still about 5%. And the prudent investor should not expect any further expansion of earnings and dividend multiples. Adding the two numbers gives an expected return on common stock of only about 6.3% versus the 6.0% percent coupon on long bonds. Thus, over the next few decades, stock returns should be only slightly higher than bond returns.

Simply put, the current optimism surrounding stock investing does not appear to be well-founded. (In fact, in 1998 the expected return of corporate bonds calculated in this manner briefly exceeded that of stocks.)

The famous financial analyst Benjamin Graham once said that in the short run the stock market is a voting machine, but that in the long run it is a weighing machine. What it weighs are earnings. In these ebullient times, the torpid and occasionally stuttering growth of common stock earnings cannot be stressed strongly enough. For this reason, I've plotted the earnings of the Dow Jones Industrial Average from 1920. Figure 2-11 shows earnings in nominal dollars, with no adjustment for inflation. The graph slopes upward at about 5% per year. Figure 2-12 shows the same data in inflation-adjusted dollars, relative to the value of a dollar in 1920. (To convert to 2000 dollars, multiply by 9.) It slopes upward at only about 2% per year. It is illogical to expect the value of a broad index of U.S. stocks to significantly exceed this "natural" real growth rate of 2%. To this return can be added your dividends. To expect more is folly.

It is more difficult to perform a similar analysis for other asset classes. It appears that the expected returns of European and Japanese stocks should be about the same as for U.S. stocks. U.S. small stocks should have somewhat higher returns. Pacific Rim and emerging markets stocks currently yield about 3% to 4%. They may also have growth rates higher than in the United States and thus may have higher returns—but of course with much higher risk. The greatest anomaly of all, however, is with REITs, which are currently yielding an almost unbelievable 8.8%. Even if they experience no earnings growth, their returns should be higher than the S&P 500.

And, to round things off, the T-bill return is almost impossible to forecast, since its "coupon" (strictly speaking, it has none, as T-bills are sold at a discount and mature at par) changes from month to month.

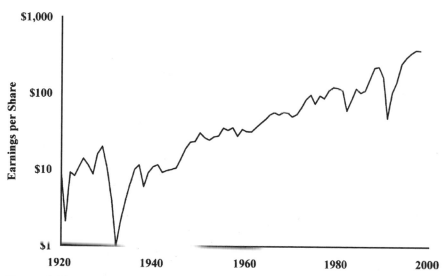

Figure 2-11. Dow Jones nominal earnings.

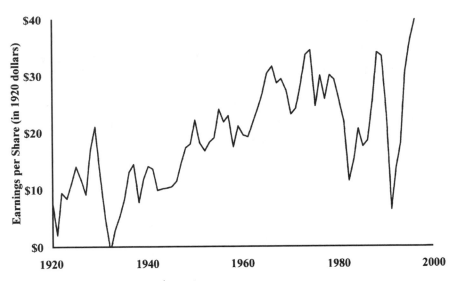

Figure 2-12. Dow Jones real earnings.

So, as the famous test pilot Chuck Yeager would say, we've got a little problem here; future stock returns estimated by the discounted dividend model are considerably lower than historical returns. What is the intelligent investor to do?

There is no right answer to this dilemma, but I would err on the conservative side and go with the discounted dividend model. Using this method, it should be possible for you to calculate your long-term *expected* investment return based on your investment choices, or "asset allocation policy." You should also be able to estimate the risk that you are taking to achieve this return.

As already alluded to, the most useful way to estimate your expected return is as inflation-adjusted, or "real," return. This will in turn simplify your retirement calculations, as the effects of inflation have already been discounted. Projecting a 4% stock return in real dollars is easier than projecting a 7% nominal return and adjusting for a 3% inflation rate, particularly when your withdrawals may be spread over 15 to 30 years. Table 2-3 provides a handy "back-of-the-envelope" summary to help you plan your finances. You say you can tolerate a 25% bear market hit as long as it occurs only once in your life? Fine. Using the percentages in Table 2-3, let's construct a portfolio consisting of 50% stock, split between large and small

Table 2-3. Expected Asset Class Characteristics

Asset	Expected inflation-adjusted return (%)	Worst bear market loss (%)
T-bills	0–3	None
All other high-quality bonds	3	None (short duration) 10 (long duration)
Large company stocks, U.S. and foreign	4	40–50
REITS, small company stocks, U.S. and foreign; emerging markets stocks	6	50–60
Precious metals stocks	0–4*	50–60

*Author's best estimate.

companies, and 50% bonds of short duration. This will lose about 25% in a once-in-a-lifetime bear market. Your inflation-adjusted portfolio expected return can be calculated as follows:

1. 25% of your portfolio in small stocks: .25 × 6% = 1.5%

2. 25% of your portfolio in large stocks: .25 × 4% = 1.0%

3. 50% of your portfolio in bonds: .5 × 3% = 1.5%

Thus, the real long-term expected return of your portfolio is:

$$1.5\% + 1\% + 1.5\% = 4\%$$

This means that you will about double the real value of your portfolio every 18 years. (This is easily calculated from "the rule of 72," which says that the return rate multiplied by the time it takes to double your assets will equal 72. In other words, at 6% return your capital will double every 12 years.)

Take another break. Don't look at this book for at least a few more days. In the next chapter we shall explore the strange and wondrous behavior of portfolios.

Summary

1. Risk and reward are inextricably intertwined. Do not expect high returns without high risk. Do not expect safety without correspondingly low returns.

2. The longer a risky asset is held, the less the chance of a poor result.

3. The risk of an asset or a portfolio can be measured. The easiest way to do this is by calculating the standard deviation of returns for many time periods.

4. Those who are ignorant of investment history are bound to repeat its mistakes. Historical investment returns and risks of various asset classes should be studied. Investment results for an asset over a long enough period (greater than 20 years) are a good guide to the future returns and risks of that asset. Further, it should be possible to approximate the future long-term return and risk of a portfolio consisting of such assets.

3

The Behavior of
Multiple-Asset Portfolios

Uncle Fred Makes You Another Offer

Time passes. You have spent several more years in the employ of
your Uncle Fred, and you have truly grown to dread the annual coin-
toss sessions. The laws of probability have served you well by
providing you with an equal number of heads and tails.
Unfortunately, your success and seniority mean that the stakes on
each coin toss grow progressively higher. Remember, at the end of
each year Uncle Fred adds $5000 to your retirement fund and
determines with a coin toss whether your return on the whole
account is a gain of 30% (heads) or a loss of 10% (tails). An ever-
growing amount of money rides on each toss, and your uncle senses
your increasing discomfort.

He makes you another offer. At the end of each year, he will divide
your pension account into two equal parts and conduct a separate
coin toss for each half.

Just what is your wily uncle up to? Your first instinct is to recoil in
horror—if one coin toss unnerves you, surely two must be worse.
However, you have an analytical frame of mind, and you begin to
dissect his proposition. You realize that there are four possible
outcomes for two coin tosses, each with an equal probability:

Outcome	First coin toss	Second coin toss	Total return
1	Heads	Heads	+30%
2	Heads	Tails	+10%
3	Tails	Heads	+10%
4	Tails	Tails	−10%

Outcomes 1 and 4 are the same as they would be in a single coin toss, with the original returns of +30% and −10%, respectively. However, there are two additional possible outcomes, in which the two tosses result in one head and one tail. The total return in these cases is 10% (one-half of +30% plus one-half of −10%).

Since each of the four possible outcomes is equally likely, and in a representative four-year period you will have one of each outcome, you find that your account will increase by a factor of:

$$1.3 \times 1.1 \times 1.1 \times .9 = 1.4157$$

Being handy with numbers, you calculate that your annualized return for this two-coin-toss sequence is 9.08%, which is nearly a full percentage point higher than your previous expected return of 8.17% with only one coin toss. Even more amazingly, you realize that your risk has been reduced—with the addition of two returns at the mean of 10%, your calculated standard deviation is now only 14.14%, as opposed to 20% for the single coin toss.

Wise old Uncle Fred has introduced you to the most important concept in portfolio theory:

> **Dividing your portfolio between assets with uncorrelated results increases return while decreasing risk.**

This seems too good to be true. The keyword here is *uncorrelated;* the result of the first coin toss in no way influences the result of the second toss. Think about it—if the two coin tosses were perfectly correlated and the second coin toss always gave the same result as the first, then we would get only the original +30% and −10% returns.

Math Details

Those of you with sophisticated investment backgrounds know that a put option on a security or a futures contract sold short will have a highly negative correlation with the return of its underlying asset. However, in that instance the two positions will have nearly opposite returns, with a near zero total portfolio return. A more precise statement would be that two assets with *positive* returns should not have persistent highly negative correlations.

We would be back to the original single coin toss, with its lower return and higher risk. If the second coin toss were perfectly *inversely* correlated with the first and always gave the opposite result, then our return would always be 10%. In this case, we would have a 10% annualized long-term return with zero risk! The point cannot be stated strongly enough: *mixing assets with uncorrelated returns reduces risk*, because when one of the assets is zigging, it is likely that the other is zagging.

In the real world of investing, it is occasionally possible to find two stock or bond classes which have zero correlation, producing a percent or so increase in return and a moderate reduction in risk. Rest assured, however, that in the long run, meaningful negative (inverse) correlations are never seen—this *would* simply be too good to be true.

Modeling the Behavior of Simple Portfolios

The coin-toss example should convince you of the value of diversifying your assets. In the real world of investing, you are faced with a seemingly limitless choice of assets which can be combined into a literally infinite number of portfolios. Yet, for each level of risk you choose to bear, there is only a single "right" mix of assets that will result in the maximum investment return. Even worse, the right, or optimal, asset mix becomes apparent only in retrospect; the optimal mix for the next 20 years is unlikely to look anything like the optimal mix for the past 20 years. How on God's green earth do you find the best future asset mix?

In order to find the answer, we begin by setting up a "laboratory" which will simulate the performance of complex portfolios. To better understand this, we shall start with some very simple examples.

Example 1. The model consists of only two assets: The first asset, Uncle Fred's coin toss, with equally likely returns of +30% and −10%, which we shall call stock in this example; and a second asset, with equally likely returns of 0% and +10%, which we shall call bond. Stock has long-term return and risk characteristics similar to those of common stocks, and bond has long-term return and risk characteristics similar to those of five-year Treasury notes. There are four possible outcomes:

Period	1	2	3	4
Stock return	+30	+30	−10	−10
Bond return	+10	0	+10	0

You are allowed to choose long-term investment in any combination of these two assets, from 100% stock to 100% bond, with any combination in between. At the end of each year you must rebalance your portfolio back to this combination. Let's assume that you pick a 50/50 mix of stock and bond. In other words, at the end of each year, 50% of your portfolio is subject to the 0 or +10 (bond) coin toss, and the other 50% is subject to the +30 or −10 (stock) coin toss. If the bond returns +10% and the stock returns −10% for a given year, at the end of that year you now have more bond than stock, and you must sell some bond and use the proceeds to buy more stock. In those years when stock returns 30%, you must similarly exchange enough stock for bond to reset the mix back to 50/50. The reasons for this are several. First and foremost, rebalancing increases long-term portfolio return while reducing risk. Second, failure to rebalance a portfolio of stocks and bonds eventually leads to an almost all-stock portfolio, because of the higher long-term returns of stock, resetting your return-risk combination to a higher level. Last, and most important, the habit of rebalancing instills in the investor the discipline necessary to buy low and sell high.

In this same example, now assume that you have chosen a portfolio of one-quarter (25%) bond and three-quarters (75%) stock. Where R_b and R_s are the returns of bond and stock, respectively, the return for this portfolio in any given period is:

$$(.25 \times R_b) + (.75 \times R_s)$$

Thus, if in a given period the stock return is +30% and the bond return is +10%, then the portfolio return is:

$$(.25 \times 10) + (.75 \times 30) = 25\%$$

The returns for each of the four possible outcomes are:

Period	1	2	3	4
Stock return	+30	+30	−10	−10
Bond return	+10	0	+10	0
Return for 75% stock, 25% bond mix	+25	+22.5	−5	−7.5

The annualized return for this portfolio is 7.70%, and its SD is 15.05%. First, note that the return of this portfolio is only 0.47% lower than 100% stock, and yet its risk (SD) is decreased by almost 5%. (Put another way, one-quarter of the risk has been eliminated at a cost of only one-seventeenth of the return.) This is simply another demonstration of the benefits of diversification. This paradigm provides you with a simple yet powerful way to study the risk-versus-return characteristics of the most common diversification tool: the stock and bond combination. Those of you who are familiar with spreadsheets will recognize that a simple file analyzing the risk and return from the above paradigm can be written in a few minutes. In Figure 3-1, these values are plotted in a manner identical to Figures 2-9 and 2-10. Remember, as you move up the graph, return increases. As we move from left to right, risk increases.

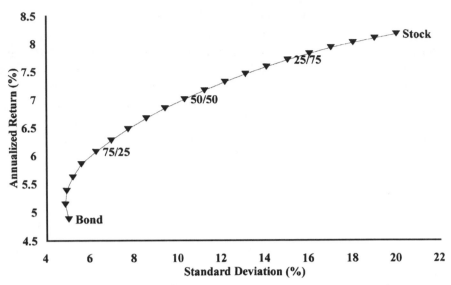

Figure 3-1. Risk versus reward.

The right side of the graph is not terribly surprising; as you add in small amounts of bond to the stock, there is a dramatic reduction of risk (SD) with a relatively small loss of return. However, the behavior of the left side of the graph is truly remarkable. If you start with an all-bond portfolio, adding small amounts of stock increases return, as expected. However, adding a small amount of stock also *decreases* the portfolio risk slightly, with the "minimum risk" portfolio consisting of about 7% stock. A stock position of 12% produces the same risk as the all-bond portfolio. *Thus, the investor whose sole aim is to minimize risk must of necessity own some stock.* This is a phenomenon we shall encounter repeatedly in our study of portfolio behavior.

Example 2. Let's perform a similar exercise for Uncle Fred's two-coin-toss portfolio at the beginning of the chapter, where two different assets return either +30% or −10%, and where each asset's return is independent of the other. To summarize:

Asset	Period 1	Period 2	Period 3	Period 4
A	+30	+30	−10	−10
B	+30	−10	+30	−10

Figure 3-2 graphs the return and risk of a portfolio of different mixes of A and B, in the same fashion as was done for Example 1. Since both assets have the same return and SD, you need to plot only half of the points, since a 75/25 mix of A/B will behave the same as a 25/75 mix. The results are clear-cut. The risk lessens (you move toward the left) and return increases (you move up) as you move toward a 50/50 mix. Each point on the graph represents a 5% change in composition, and you can see that most of the gain in return versus risk occurs as you move from 100% of either asset to a 75/25 composition. The trip from 75/25 to 50/50 produces much less additional benefit. The risk and benefit of a 65/35 mix does not differ significantly from the 50/50 mix—less than 0.1% of return and 0.5% of SD. This example makes these key points:

1. If two assets have similar long-term returns and risks and are not perfectly correlated, then investing in a fixed, rebalanced mix of the two not only reduces risk but also actually increases return. You already know that the reduced risk is the result of the imperfect correlation between the two assets; a bad result for one asset is quite likely to be associated with a good result for the other, mitigating

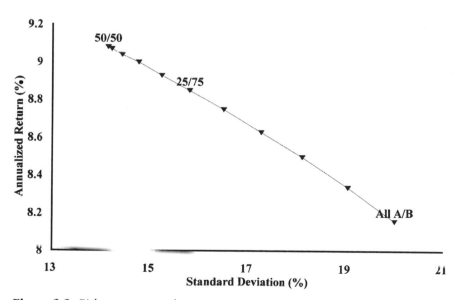

Figure 3-2. Risk versus reward.

your loss. The increased return is another facet of the same phe-nomenon: If a good result for one asset is associated with a bad result for the other, then the rebalancing requirement forces you to sell some of the successful asset (sell high) in order to buy more of the unsuccessful asset (buy low). This excess return is not obtained with-out rebalancing.

2. If two poorly correlated assets have similar returns and risks, then the optimal mix of the two will be close to 50/50.

3. There is plenty of margin for error available in asset allocation policy. If you are off 10% or 20% from what in retrospect turned out to be the best allocation, you have not lost that much. As we shall see, sticking by your asset allocation policy through thick and thin is much more important than picking the "best" allocation.

Dealing with More Than Two Imperfectly Correlated Assets

The above models have been quite useful for demonstrating the effect of diversification on risk and return of two similar assets (Example 2) and two different assets (Example 1) with zero correlation. Unfortunately, the above examples are no more than useful illustrations of the theoretical benefits of diversified portfolios. In the real world of investing, we must deal with mixes of dozens of asset types, each with a different return and risk. Even worse, the returns of these assets are only rarely completely uncorrelated. Worse still, the risks, returns, and correlations of these assets fluctuate considerably over time. In order to understand real portfolios, we shall require much more complex techniques.

Thus far we have dealt with portfolios with only two uncorrelated components. Two uncorrelated assets may be represented with four time periods as in Uncle Fred's coin toss, three assets with eight periods, four assets with 16 periods, etc. In the real world of investing, however, it is difficult to find two assets that are uncorrelated, and it is practically impossible to find three. It is absolutely impossible to find more than three mutually uncorrelated assets. The reason for this is simple. A portfolio of two assets has only one correlation. Three assets have three correlations, and four assets have six correlations.

(This is the same reason why big offices have messier politics than small ones. A three-person office has three interpersonal relationships; a 10-person office has 45 relationships.)

Real assets are almost always *imperfectly* correlated. In other words, an above-average return in one is somewhat more likely to be associated with an above-average return in the other. The degree of correlation is expressed by a *correlation coefficient.* This value ranges from −1 to +1. Perfectly correlated assets have a correlation coefficient of +1, and uncorrelated assets have a coefficient of 0. *Perfectly inversely* (or negatively) correlated assets have a coefficient of −1. The easiest way to understand this is to plot the returns of two assets against each other for many periods, as is done in Figures 3-3, 3-4, and 3-5.

Each figure plots the 288 monthly returns for each asset pair for the 24-year period from January 1975 to December 1998. Each point on the graph represents the return for one of those months; the return for the first asset is read on the x (horizontal) axis, and for the second asset on the y (vertical) axis. If the assets are perfectly correlated, they will all fit on a straight line. (If the correlation is positive, the line will run from lower-left to upper-right; if negative, the line will run from upper-left to lower-right.) If they are uncorrelated, they will be widely scattered.

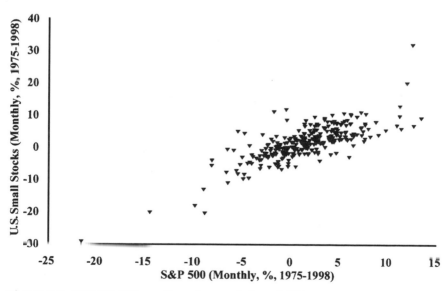

Figure 3-3. S&P 500/U.S. small stock, correlation of .777.

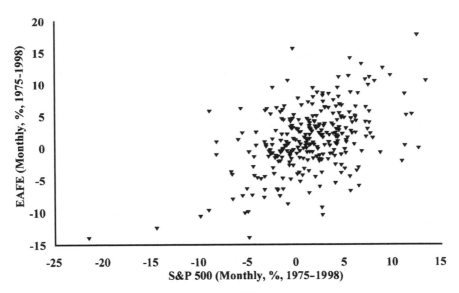

Figure 3-4. S&P 500/EAFE, correlation of .483.

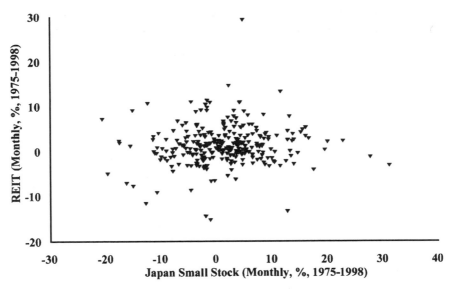

Figure 3-5. Japan small stock/REIT correlation of .068.

Figure 3-3 plots the monthly returns for 1975–1998 of the S&P 500 versus U.S. small stocks. Most of the points lie on nearly a straight line; a poor return for one was invariably associated with a poor return for the other. The correlation coefficient of .777 for these two assets is quite high. This graph demonstrates that adding U.S. small stocks to a portfolio of U.S. large stocks does not diminish risk very much, as a poor return for one will be very likely associated with a poor return for the other.

Figure 3-4 plots two loosely correlated assets—U.S. large stocks (S&P 500) and foreign large stocks (EAFE Index). Although there does appear to be a loose relation between the two, it is far from perfect. The correlation coefficient of this pair is .483.

Lastly, Figure 3-5 plots two very poorly correlated assets (correlation coefficient of .068): Japanese small stocks and REITs. This plot is a "scattergram" with no discernable pattern. A good or bad result for one of these assets tells us nothing about the result for the other.

Why is this so important? As already discussed the most diversification benefit is obtained from uncorrelated assets. The above

---

Math Details: How to Calculate a Correlation Coefficient

In this book's previous versions, I included a section on the manual calculation of the correlation coefficient. In the personal computer age, this is an exercise in masochism. The easiest way to do this is with a spreadsheet. Let's assume that you have 36 monthly returns for two assets, A and B. Enter the returns in columns A and B, next to each other, spanning rows 1 to 36 for each pair of values.

In Excel, enter in a separate cell the formula = CORREL(A1:A36, B1:B36)

In Quattro Pro, the formula would be @CORREL(A1..A36, B1..B36)

Both of these packages also contain a tool that will calculate a "correlation grid" of all of the correlations of an array of data for more than two assets. Those of you who would like an explanation of the steps involved in calculating a correlation coefficient are referred to a standard statistics text.

analysis suggests that there is not much benefit from mixing domestic small and large stocks and that there is great benefit from mixing REITs and Japanese small stocks. In the real world of investing, this turns out to be the case.

Summary

1. The concept of correlation of assets is central to portfolio theory—the lower the correlation, the better.

2. Diversifying your portfolio among uncorrelated assets reduces risk and increases return. It is necessary to rebalance your portfolio periodically to capture this increased return.

4

The Behavior of
Real-World Portfolios

So far we've explored two of the critical building blocks of investment theory: the behavior of single classes of stocks and bonds and the behavior of very simple model portfolios. It is time to examine the behavior of portfolios of actual stocks and bonds. We shall then begin to approach the central question of portfolio analysis: *What portfolios produce the most return for the least amount of risk?*

Examining the Behavior of Complex Portfolios: The Return-Risk Plot

Thus far, we have dealt only with simple portfolios having two components with zero correlation. A "complex" portfolio is one with many components whose correlations vary widely. And, unfortunately, correlations are rarely zero; you can expect to see values anywhere between 0 and 1, with most values clustering between .3 and .8. These are the sorts of portfolios you encounter in the real world. It is not hard to study, or "model," the behavior of complex portfolios if you approach the problem methodically. Let's take the two most commonly used risky assets: large company stocks and long-term duration (20-year) U.S. Treasury bonds. The annual returns of these assets are available from the Ibbotson SBBI, discussed in Chapter 2. Assume that we wish to study the behavior of a 50/50 mix of these two assets. For any given year, the return for this portfolio is the sum of each individual return times its portfolio composition, in this case .5. If the return of stocks for a given year is 24% and the return of bonds is 2%, a 50/50 mix has a return of:

$$(.5 \times 24\%) + (.5 \times 2\%) = 12\% + 1\% = 13\%$$

For a 60/40 mix the return is:

$$(.6 \times 24\%) + (.4 \times 2\%) = 14.4\% + .8\% = 15.2\%$$

We can calculate the portfolio return for any given asset mix for each of the 73 years between 1926 and 1998. An annualized return and SD for each portfolio can be computed from these 73 annual portfolio returns. Sound tedious? It is if you are doing it by hand. Those of you familiar with computers and spreadsheets will recognize that a file that performs this task can be written in a matter of minutes. You can easily write a spreadsheet file in such a way that you have to enter only the portfolio composition, and the return and SD data instantly appear for that mix. (For those who are interested, a sample spreadsheet file is available at http://www.efficientfrontier.com/files/sample.exe.)

We start with 100% stock, then a 95/5 mix of stock/bond, then 90/10, then 85/15, and so on, all the way to 100% bond. The spreadsheet will compute the annualized returns and SDs as fast as the portfolio compositions are keyed in. You can use the same spreadsheet software to plot each of the 21 portfolio compositions on an *x–y* graph, using SD for the *x* value and annualized return for the *y* value. The result is displayed in Figure 4-1.

Such graphs are essential to your understanding of investment strategy. You have seen similar graphs in the previous chapters. Remember, as we travel up the graph, return increases, and as we travel to the right, risk increases.

The triangles (plotted points) are connected, and we can travel along the described path. Let us start at the bottom left, at the point labeled "100% Bond." We travel from this point toward the "stock" point in the upper right of the graph. The path initially heads nearly straight up. This means that adding the first 15% (three ticks) or so of stock adds no risk at all, while the return is increased. As we add another 10% (two ticks) or so of stock, the path starts to curve slightly to the right, meaning that further increases in return are accompanied

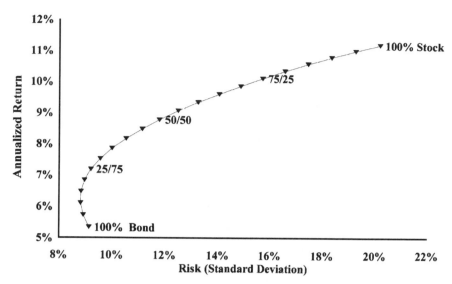

Figure 4-1. Stock/20-year Treasury mixes, 1926–1998.

by a slight increase in risk. By the time we are past the 50/50 mark, the addition of more stock to the mix adds only slightly to the return, while increasing the risk considerably. Looked at from another perspective, one can start from the other end, at "100% Stock." From this points, the path heads almost straight to the left. Adding a small amount of bonds to stock dramatically reduces risk at almost no cost in return. Note that the plot of the return-versus-risk data for the various stock and bond mixes in Figure 4-1 describes a curve with a slight upward bulge, which tells us that we are getting extra return from our diversification. Also, at the extreme left of the curve there is a more prominent bulge to the left, which tells us that there is a significant reduction in risk to be had by adding a small amount of stock to an all-bond portfolio. You will see more such curves in the coming pages. You can gauge the diversification benefit of any asset pair by the amount of bulge the curve exhibits. The more bulge, the better.

You may recognize that Figure 4-1 looks almost like Figure 3-1 in the previous chapter. Recall that this is derived from Example 1, the stock-bond paradigm. It is remarkable that such a simple model so accurately describes the behavior of stocks and bonds in the real world.

Recollect that the 1926–1998 Ibbotson database contains other assets as well, including U.S. Treasury obligations of shorter maturity, as well as those wild and wooly small stocks. It is a simple matter to add them to our spreadsheet and produce return-versus-risk plots for them.

Figure 4-2 contains the same kind of stock and 20-year bond plot as Figure 4-1, except that we have two more bond choices: 30-day T-bills and 5-year Treasury notes. The three different curves represent the mixture of stocks and 20-year bonds, stocks and 5-year notes, and stocks and 30-day T-bills. What does this tell us? First, look at the right half of the graph. The three curves are really quite close together at this point. Assume you can tolerate high portfolio risk, say at the level of a 15% SD. To obtain a portfolio with this level of risk you will be diluting your stock with only a small amount of bond, and it really doesn't matter which of the three different bonds you use. Your return and risk will be the same. Next assume that you can tolerate only 10% SD of risk. Clearly, at this level the use of 5-year notes is superior to the other two bond choices; over most of its extent it lies above the other two curves, indicating that for each degree of risk the 5-year notes and stock mix yields more return. Only at low risk levels is the use of T-bills desirable. Portfolio simulations with other databases using both backtesting and another technique called *mean-variance*

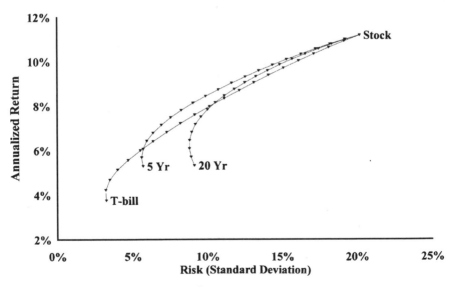

Figure 4-2. Stock/bond mixes, 1926–1998.

analysis also suggest the superiority of short-term bonds. On occasion it may be advantageous to use long-term bonds or T-bills in small amounts. In general, however, you will not go far wrong by sticking to bond maturities of six months to five years for the risk-diluting portion of your portfolio.

The Ibbotson database contains two other assets: small stocks and long-term corporate bonds. The small company stocks behave similarly to large stocks, and long-term corporate bonds behave nearly identically to 20-year Treasury bonds.

Risk Dilution

If you are unhappy with the degree of risk in your portfolio, you have two ways to reduce it. The first way is to employ less risky individual assets. An example of this would be to substitute large stocks for small stocks, domestic stocks for foreign stocks, or utility stocks for industrial stocks. The second way is to stick with your basic allocation among stock groups and simply replace a small amount of your entire stock allocation with a like amount of short-term bonds. In doing so you are traveling from right to left on the return-risk curve, lowering your risk and return at the same time. *Risk dilution* refers to this process of traveling from right to left on a return-versus-risk curve.

If you believe that you have found an effective stock allocation, it is generally a better idea to employ risk dilution, as this leaves your chosen stock strategy undisturbed. Reshuffling your overall stock strategy is likely to result in a less effective portfolio. As we have already seen, a conservative, risk-averse investment strategy will almost always involve at least a small amount of exposure to very risky individual assets. This is seen in the left-hand portions of Figures 4-1 and 4-2; the addition of a small amount of large (or small) stocks to a 100% bond portfolio actually reduces risk slightly. Start with the first data point on the left of these graphs, indicating the all-bond portfolio. Proceeding up the next few points, as one adds in a small amount of stocks all of the curves initially travel both up, indicating higher return, and to the *left*, indicating slightly *lower* risk. Only as one adds in still more stock does the curve move off to the right, indicating higher risk. The stock composition of a high-risk portfolio usually does not differ much from that of a low-risk portfolio. The main difference is in the broad allocation between stocks and bonds.

Foreign Assets

Recall the two-coin-toss model discussed in Chapter 3. The extra return obtained from having the returns for each half of your portfolio determined by different coin tosses depends upon the results of the two coin tosses being independent of each other, i.e., uncorrelated. If the two coin tosses were always the same (highly correlated), there would be no advantage to the two-coin-toss model. *The essence of effective portfolio construction is the use of a large number of poorly correlated assets.* Unfortunately, the all-U.S. 1926–1998 database contains only two broad categories that do not correlate well: stocks and bonds. The correlation of large and small stocks with each other is quite high, as is the correlation of intermediate and long bonds. It is necessary to use foreign securities if we wish to construct a portfolio containing many imperfectly correlated components. Good-quality data for foreign stock and bond returns are available after 1969. This is fortunate, as the worst bear market of modern times occurred in 1973–1974. Examination of portfolio behavior in these years yields a good measurement of bear-market risk.

A decade ago one often heard about the high returns available from foreign investing. By 1985 you couldn't look at the "Money and Investing" section of *The Wall Street Journal* without reading about how the managers of large pension funds, endowments, and private pools were increasing their foreign exposure to capture this high return. Financial gurus of all stripes discoursed learnedly on the amount of exposure allotted to foreign assets.

The most widely available foreign stock index is the Morgan Stanley Europe, Australasia, and Far East Index, commonly known as the EAFE (pronounced "eef' ah"). For the 20-year period ending 1988, EAFE returns *were* about 2% higher than comparable U.S. equity returns for both large and small stocks. (At that time, foreign bonds also had higher returns than their domestic counterparts by about the same margin.) The 1969–1988 20-year return-versus-risk plot for S&P 500 and EAFE mixes is shown in Figure 4-3. Talk about a free lunch! Start at the bottom of the curve. Each increment of added EAFE

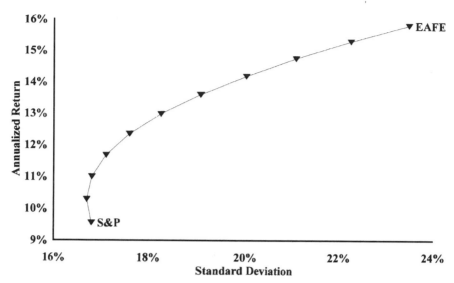

Figure 4-3. S&P 500/EAFE mixes, 1969–1988.

exposure increased return, and the first few notches actually decreased risk. Add 30% EAFE to your fuddy-duddy domestic stocks and you get 2% more annualized return with almost no extra risk.

Does this sound too good to be true? Well, it is. Let's see what the *last* 20 years looked like, from 1979 to 1998, in Figure 4-4. Goodbye free lunch. Although the first two notches of EAFE decrease risk, they also decrease return. And after that, it's steeply downhill for both risk and return. In 2000, as this book is being written, what are the gurus telling us? "Stay at home for higher returns. Buy the companies you know. Diversify abroad only at your peril. And, if you must invest abroad, do so only where you can drink the water."

A small digression. I'll talk about the field of behavioral finance later in the book, but this is a perfect example of so-called *recency*, the single biggest mistake that even the most experienced investors make. This refers to our tendency to extrapolate recent trends indefinitely into the future. In more formal terms, it refers to overemphasis on recent, but incomplete data and the dismissal of older, but more complete data. It is human nature to weigh most heavily *recent* dramatic events. Readers of a certain age will vividly remember the great inflationary period of the 1970s and early 1980s. At the time, it was difficult to imagine this economic scourge ever ending. The only

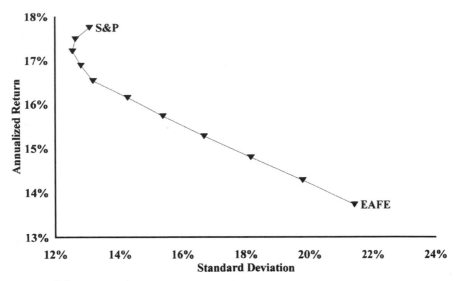

Figure 4-4. S&P 500/EAFE mixes, 1979–1998.

assets to own were real estate and gold. And if you were unfortunate enough to be holding what were derisively known as "paper assets," (stocks and bonds), you had your head handed to you. More readers will remember the mixed feeling of dread and awe of Japanese economic prowess a decade ago. The United States' real estate crown jewels were being purchased like so many detergent boxes at a "blue-light special," and our great manufacturing concerns seemed unable to compete with Tokyo's corporate juggernaut.

In both cases, investment decisions based on these perceptions would have been disastrous. Both Japanese stocks and precious metals have since been horrid investments. A recurring theme in these pages is that you try as hard as you can to identify the diverse strains of current financial wisdom in order that you may *ignore them.*

Now that we've ascertained that the popular view of international diversification has been poisoned by the recent poor performance of foreign stocks, what does the "complete" data show? Figure 4-5 is the risk-return plot for the full 30-year period from 1969 to 1998. For this period the returns for the S&P (12.67%) and EAFE (12.39%) were nearly identical. Note also how narrowly spaced the return values on the *y* axis are, with less than 1% separating all of the portfolio returns.

Note how "bulgy" this plot is. Portfolios of up to 80% EAFE have higher returns than either asset alone. Portfolios of up to 40% EAFE also have less risk than either asset alone. There can be no question that for the past 30 years international diversification has worked superbly.

How complete is even the 30-year data? Good question. Remember that the years from 1914 to 1945 were not terribly kind to many equity markets. The bourses of Japan and Germany were essentially obliterated by war, and almost the entire private sectors of numerous other nations in Latin America and Eastern Europe were expropriated by colonels and apparatchiks who didn't pay enough attention in Economics 101. Two academics, Will Goetzmann of Yale and Phillipe Jorion of the University of California, Irvine, have looked at returns after 1920 outside of the United States and have tried to measure the damage wrought by these "market extinctions" on a global investment strategy. They found that the United States had the world's highest equity returns, about 8% over inflation, with Canada, the United Kingdom, Switzerland, Sweden, and Australia fairly close behind. However, many other nations, particularly countries that we would now term "emerging markets," had much lower returns, some negative in real terms. If you do read this paper, listed in the

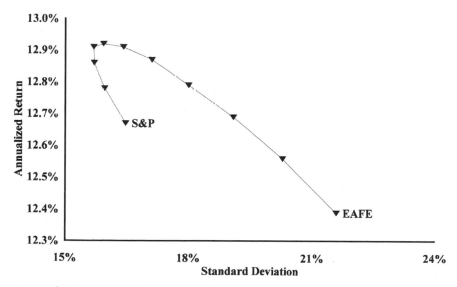

Figure 4-5. S&P 500/EAFE mixes, 1969–1998.

Bibliography, be aware that the returns presentation is very confusing. Returns are reported in inflation-adjusted terms, with dividends not included. Thus, the U.S. return is reported at about 4%. To this must be added an average 4% dividend (for a total real return of 8%) plus another 3% for inflation, for a total nominal return of 11%.

The main point of the Jorion-Goetzmann work is that the careful investor must be aware of so-called survivorship bias. That is, it is easy to look just at U.S. returns and conclude that long-term real returns will continue to be high. However, the United States has been the winner in the global equity sweepstakes; the returns in most other markets have not been nearly as high. Of course, there is no guarantee that the United States will continue winning. Moreover, it is easy to look at the S&P and EAFE and be encouraged by their high returns. But these two indexes constitute the "survivors." Had you started by looking at all of the markets extant in 1920, you would find that many of them disappeared, and your total global return would have been much lower. The same is no doubt true today as well. It is by no means certain that even today's largest markets will be in business 30 years from now. Remember that in 1930 some of the world's biggest bourses were located in Berlin, Cairo, and Buenos Aires.

Jorion and Goetzmann's conclusions about global investing are reasonably upbeat, however. They found that a global portfolio weighted according to national gross domestic product returned about 1% less than a domestic portfolio, but also had a much lower standard deviation. They concluded that the main advantage of international diversification was not increased return but decreased risk. This is borne out by looking at the 1930s and 1970s, which were brutal bear markets in the United States. During both periods, losses were less elsewhere, benefiting the global investor.

Just as investors a decade ago were overly optimistic about foreign diversification, investors today are overly pessimistic about it. Foreign stocks belong in everyone's portfolio.

Another Visit with Uncle Fred

Your benevolent uncle has taken an interest in your exploration of portfolio theory and senses your discomfort concerning foreign stock exposure. The two of you discuss Figures 4-3 through 4-5 and wrestle with their meaning. By now you know that Uncle Fred never provides a direct answer to your problems.

You don't know what to make of such disparate data. Figure 4-3 shows that heavily weighting foreign over domestic stocks is clearly advantageous, Figure 4-4 shows the exact opposite, and Figure 4-5 indicates that healthy amounts of both are needed.

"Well," says your wise old uncle, "since you can't predict equity returns, why don't you try splitting the difference? Also remember, young man, you aren't going to invest all of your savings in stocks."

So, you go back to your spreadsheet and come up with Figure 4-6. This displays the problem as well as the solution. It shows the risk-return plot for the two overlapping 20-year time periods. The thin-lined "sail" is the earlier period, and the thick-lined sail is the later period. The plot for each period contains three basic stock mixes: S&P only, EAFE only, and a 50/50 mix of both. For each period, all three of these are then mixed with five-year Treasury notes, which are the two points in the lower left of the graph on which all three lines for each period converge.

First, notice that returns in general were much higher in the later period. In fact, for the earlier period the return of the S&P was not much greater than that of the five-year note. And this plot does not

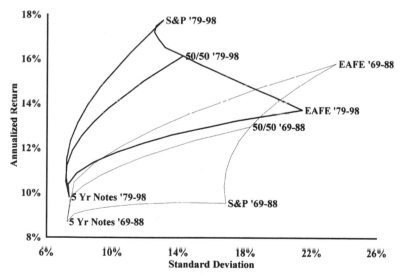

Figure 4-6. S&P 500/EAFE, 1979–1988.

show the most discouraging thing about the 1969–1988 period; inflation was almost 7%, so the real returns of both domestic stocks and bonds were nearly zero. Inflation in the later period was nearly 2% lower, with real returns being correspondingly higher.

This graph is a good study in "recency." In 1988, everybody and their dogs were enthusiastic about foreign equity, as it had much higher returns than domestic equity. More importantly, enthusiasm for stocks in general was not particularly high, so 1988 was a great year to sell your foreign stocks and buy domestic equity.

Now, look at the more recent (upper, heavier-lined) period. U.S. equity returns have been quite high, and "everybody knows" that stocks have the highest investment returns, particularly U.S. stocks. Recency, again. Remember Bernard Baruch's famous dictum:

Something that everyone knows isn't worth knowing.

It cannot be repeated often enough. Identify the era's conventional wisdom and then ignore it.

Now look at the individual plots in Figure 4-6. Picking the worst of the stock and bond lines in each era (S&P and bond in the earlier period, EAFE and bond in the later period) would have produced poor returns, and the best stock and bond line excellent returns. The trouble, as Yogi Berra once said, is that it's very difficult to make predictions, particularly about the future. If you take your uncle's advice and split the difference, you find that you do reasonably well in both eras. In both cases the return of the 50/50 line is much closer to the best-performing asset line than the worst-performing asset line. And for the entire 30-year period, we already know that the 50/50 mix is in itself the "best" equity asset.

Almost all of the foreign stock advantage of the earlier 1969–1988 period came from currency gain, as rises in the yen and European currencies provided U.S. investors with about 2% of extra return. And, the reversal in fortunes in the foreign-versus-domestic pony race of the past 20 years may turn out to be equally anomalous. Who knows whether foreign or domestic stocks will have the higher return over the next 20, 30, or even 50 years? However, it seems highly likely that a 50/50 mix will not be too far from the best foreign-versus-domestic allocation. *The real purpose of portfolio backtesting, mean-variance analysis, or any other kind of portfolio analysis is not to find the "best" asset mix. Rather, it is to find a portfolio mix that will not be too far off the mark under a wide variety of circumstances.*

Small Stocks versus Large Stocks

It's important to realize how large and small stocks behave relative to each other. Until recently it was generally accepted that small stocks had higher returns than large stocks. With the recent remarkable performance of the S&P 500, the so-called small-cap premium has been questioned, although over the past 73 years this premium still seems to be about 1%. We are looking at recency again—our tendency to overemphasize recent events. However, no one questions that small stocks are more risky than large stocks. In Figure 4-7, I've plotted various mixes of small and large stocks with the ubiquitous five-year Treasury notes. First, note that the two plots nearly overlap. In other words, the risk-return curves are very

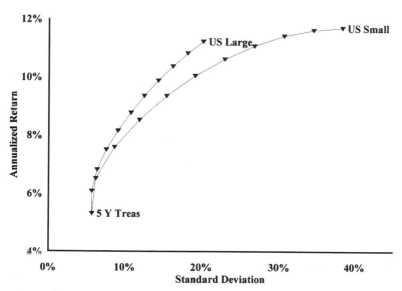

Figure 4-7. Large and small stocks/bonds, 1926–1998.

similar, except that the small-stock curve extends out a lot farther to the right than the S&P curve. In the present graph, large stock and bond mixes appear to be slightly more efficient than small stock and bond mixes. On the other hand, when the same graph, was drawn four years ago, the small-stock curve was slightly more efficient than the large-stock curve. The most important revelation in Figure 4-7, however, is that a little small stock goes a long way. Notice how in the 1926–1998 period, a 50/50 mix of small stocks and bonds has almost the same risk and return as 100% large stocks. More recent data suggests that this "potency" has decreased somewhat, perhaps to only 1.5 times that of the S&P. But the basic principle remains that you get more bang for the buck in terms of both risk and return from small stocks.

Finally, to complete the picture, small foreign stocks need to be considered. There's a problem here: the most commonly used international small-cap index is an extremely peculiar one. Constructed by Dimensional Fund Advisors, this index goes back to 1970, almost as far as the EAFE itself. Unfortunately, until 1988 it consisted of just two markets—Japan and the United Kingdom. After 1988, its composition is quite similar to the EAFE. With that caveat in mind, I've plotted the behavior of mixtures of U.S. small stocks and international small stocks for the 1970–1998 period in Figure 4-8. Note how "bulgy" this curve is. At the extreme right part of the curve, note how the addition of U.S. small stocks reduces risk with almost no loss of return. At the opposite end of the curve, the addition of large amounts of international small stocks dramatically increases return without increasing risk. Figure 4-8 paints a relatively rosy picture of global small-stock investing, but it has a dark side. I've tabulated the returns for U.S. and foreign stocks, both small and large, for the first 20 years (1970–1989) and the last nine years (1990–1998) of the 1970–1998 period:

	S&P 500	EAFE	U.S. small stocks	International small stocks
1970–1989	11.55%	16.26%	11.82%	26.14%
1990–1998	17.89%	5.29%	13.56%	−1.08%

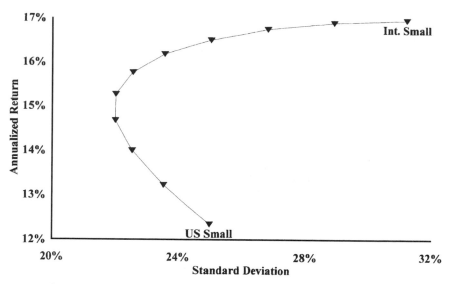

Figure 4-8. U.S./international small-stock mixes, 1970–1998.

Notice what a wild ride international small stocks have been, with staggering returns during the first period followed by truly awful returns during the second. It seems that when foreign stocks do well, foreign small stocks do especially well, and vice versa. Do they belong in your portfolio? It depends upon how much "tracking error" you can tolerate. If it bothers you greatly to temporarily do poorly while others are doing well, in spite of your good long-term returns, then they're probably not for you.

The Efficient Frontier

Notice how complicated things become with the three-asset portfolios we've discussed above. In the real world, of course, we have to deal with dozens of asset classes. There are an infinite number of ways to combine such a complex palette of ingredients. How can you possibly arrive at a reasonably efficient mixture of them?

For illustrative purposes, I've chosen six basic equity assets which are part of most global investors' portfolios (whether they know it or not): the S&P 500, U.S. small stocks, European stocks, Japanese stocks, Pacific Rim stocks, and precious metals stocks. And once

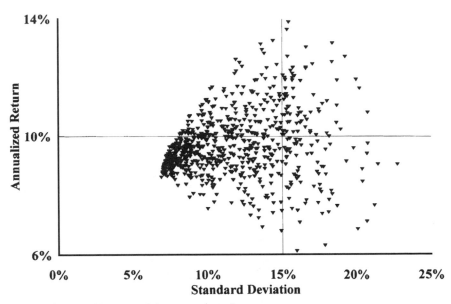

Figure 4-9. Random portfolios, 1992–1996.

again, I've chosen five-year Treasury notes for risk dilution. I (or more accurately, my colleague David Wilkinson) generated 800 random portfolios consisting of these seven assets. I then calculated the annual returns and standard deviations for these portfolios for the five-year period 1992–1996. The result, which is plotted in Figure 4-9, displays a cloud of portfolios of differing returns and risks (standard deviations).

Are some of these portfolios better than others? Absolutely. Notice that this graph is divided by a horizontal line and by a vertical line. The vertical line represents all portfolios with a standard deviation of 15%, which is about the same degree of risk as a portfolio of large U.S. stocks. Notice how some of the portfolios along this line have returns as low as 6%, whereas others have returns as high as 14%. Obviously, then, it's better to be on the top of the cloud than the bottom of the cloud. If you're going to expose yourself to risk at the 15% SD level, you might as well get the best possible return.

The horizontal line defines all portfolios with a 10% return. Notice that some of these portfolios have as little as 8% of SD, whereas others along this line have over 20% of SD. Obviously, then, it's better to be on the left side of the cloud.

Now step back and look at the entire cloud. Notice how reasonably well defined the upper left edge is. This is where we want to be—getting either the most return for a given degree of risk or being exposed to the least risk for a given return. This edge of the cloud is called the *efficient frontier*. The concept of the efficient frontier is central to portfolio theory. Unfortunately, it is also the source of more than a little mischief.

Santa Claus

Many investors and financial analysts spend a lot of time thinking about the efficient frontier. They remind me of children dreaming of Santa Claus. After all, this is the ultimate free lunch: high returns at low risk, or decent returns with almost no risk at all. There's only one problem. *There is no Santa Claus.* It's a little like trying to generate electrical power by placing a battery and a lightning rod at the last place you saw lightning strike. It isn't likely to strike there again. In other words, next year's efficient frontier will be nowhere near last year's. Anybody who tells you that their portfolio recommendations are "on the efficient frontier" also talks to Elvis and frolics with the Easter Bunny.

To illustrate this point, I had my colleague David Wilkinson generate 800 more portfolios for the same seven assets, but this time for the 27-year period from 1970 to 1996. The results are plotted in Figure 4-10. First note that the portfolio cloud is shaped quite differently from the first one—it's quite a bit flatter. This is because over short time periods annualized returns for assets tend to be quite different, but these differences tend to disappear over longer periods. In other words, over very short periods your precise stock allocation matters a great deal, but this becomes less important over very long time periods.

Much more important is what the graphs don't show. The efficient frontier portfolios for the 1992–1996 period were heavy with S&P 500 and European stocks, while the efficient frontier portfolios for the longer period are heavy with Japanese, U.S. small, and precious metals stocks. In fact, had you calculated the efficient frontier for the first half of the whole period (1970–1983) and used it to determine your portfolio for the second half of the period (1984–1996), you'd have gotten your head handed to you. The efficient-frontier portfolio of Japanese, precious metals, and U.S. small stocks for the first half would have tanked in the second half.

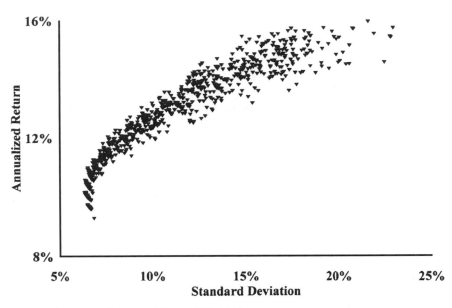

Figure 4-10. Random Portfolios, 1970–1996.

Another thing the clouds don't show is what happens when you radically alter your allocation over time. Remember that all of the above portfolio simulations I've shown you assume a *constant* allocation over the time period studied. Could you earn higher returns by picking the best performing asset for each one-year or five-year period in your analysis? Of course. It's just that this is not humanly possible. As we've already discussed, nobody consistently times the market; shifting your allocation over time is a recipe for disaster. In fact, most global investors wound up doing much worse than shown in the clouds in Figures 4-9 and 4-10 for precisely this reason.

Institutional money managers are fond of, and small investors are entranced by, so-called strategic asset allocation. What this entails is spending large sums of client money on sophisticated macroeconomic, political, and market analyses in an attempt to guess which assets will perform the best. And it's a fool's errand. Why? Because the markets have already impounded this information into the current price. You say that the U.S. economy is the world's strongest and will continue to be for the foreseeable future? That may be true, but the whole world knows it, and that is why $100 buys you only $3 earnings on Wall Street, versus $8 to $15 of earnings in Seoul,

Hong Kong, or São Paulo. Again, think recency. And the next time you see some impressive guy in a $2000 suit spinning a very plausible patter on the future direction of the economies or markets, remember that his father was probably pushing Krugerrands in 1979, and his older brother urging Japanese stocks in 1989.

The key point about the efficient frontier is this: it's a chimera, the image of your Aunt Tillie in a cloud scudding overhead a few minutes ago. And again, if somebody tells you he or she knows where it is, turn and run the other way, as fast as you can.

Still, if you're trying to capture lightning in a jar, you are better off in Texas than in Alaska. There are certain asset combinations and portfolios which are likely (but not certain) to do reasonably well.

The Importance of Rebalancing

An important assumption underlies all of the portfolio discussions thus far: that at the end of each year the investor rebalances the portfolio back to the target compositions. If a particular asset has done extraordinarily well, its portfolio weighting will increase; consequently, enough of it must be sold and reinvested in the poorly performing assets, to return to the target composition. This target composition is often referred to as the "policy allocation." You cannot underestimate the amount of discipline and patience required for this process, because it means doing exactly the opposite of what most of the investment world, almost all of whom are professionals and experts, is doing. A psychologist friend points out that this is an effective way of becoming a "contrarian," always moving in the opposite direction of the crowd. You will of necessity be selling what everybody loves and buying what they hate. You have only to remember that the great buying opportunities in U.S. stocks in 1974 and Japanese stocks in 1970, to name a few, followed several years of grinding bear markets. But be forewarned: investing during market bottoms has the distinct feel of throwing money down a rat hole.

The Experts

Small investors often consider themselves at a disadvantage with professionals who manage large sums and have access to sophisticated and timely analysis. Nothing could be further from the truth. The small investor has three overwhelming advantages over the large institutional investor:

1. She or he can aggressively rebalance a portfolio without having to deal with clients annoyed with the purchase of poorly performing assets. An oft-quoted analogy likens successful investing to driving the wrong way up a one-way street. This is difficult enough with your own vehicle. It is nearly impossible when you are a chauffeur piloting a Rolls Royce whose owner is in the back seat, squawking at every pothole and potential collision.

2. The small investor can invest in small stocks. Large institutions are effectively barred from this area by the huge sums they must invest. You can buy only so much of a small, thinly traded company before the price is bid too high to provide a reasonable return.

3. You will not be fired after a bad quarter. Even the most successful investor has dry spells, occasionally lasting years. Joe DiMaggio had slumps, and Warren Buffett occasionally gets burned. More importantly, even the most expertly crafted asset allocation will often underperform "the market," usually defined as the Dow Jones Industrial Average or the S&P 500. In fact, most successful asset allocation strategies will underperform the DJIA and S&P 500 about four years out of 10.

To illustrate this point I calculated the efficient frontier portfolios for the seven assets in Figures 4-9 and 4-10 for the entire 1970–1996 period. The best return was obtained with a mix of approximately equal parts U.S. small, Japanese, and precious metals stocks. Of course, the odds that this allocation will be that successful in the future are small—this allocation fails common sense and the "prudent man test" in every respect. Nonetheless, this particular mix outperformed the S&P by well over 3% on an annualized basis for the 1970–1996 period. And yet, *this extremely successful allocation underperformed the S&P in 12 out of the 27 years studied—i.e., 44% of the time.* I would go one step further and state that if your asset allocation never significantly underperforms the S&P 500 then you are probably doing something wrong. The professional investor with lagging performance feels enormous pressure to buy everybody else's favorite stocks. Doing so is usually a prelude to disaster.

It's easy to be impressed with glib market analyses offered in the newspaper or television. Often, while I am listening to an analyst on TV, I'll fire up Morningstar's Principia on my PC and see if he or she manages a publicly traded closed-end or open-end mutual fund. The results are instructive. A famous market analyst, credited with "calling the crash" in 1987, actually ran a mutual fund for a major investment firm that so grossly underperformed the market that it was finally folded. Another analyst, who appears regularly on an extremely well-known public television investment program, also credited with "calling the crash" in front of 20 million viewers, runs several closed-end and open-end funds whose performance can charitably be called mediocre. A noted newsletter writer who appears regularly on a prime-time public television market program has had his recommendations analyzed by a highly respected pair of academics. They found that if you actually had taken his advice, you would have lost 5.4% per year *annualized over 13 years*. And so it goes.

Just as a compulsive and unskilled gambler occasionally beats the house, so too will these "professionals" occasionally best the patient individual investor. In actual fact, it is the small investor with a fixed asset allocation policy who has an unfair advantage over the professional. The object is to develop a long-term strategy, so that you become the casino owner, not the mark.

Summary

It is possible to study the behavior of various asset mixes via the use of historical data. These techniques tell us:

1. The addition of a small amount of stock to a bond portfolio increases return while actually reducing risk slightly; even the most risk-averse investor should own some stocks.

2. The addition of a small amount of bonds to a stock portfolio significantly reduces risk while reducing return only slightly.

3. Favor short-term bonds (of six months to five years) as your "risk diluting" asset, rather than long-term bonds.

4. Small stocks have to be diluted with more bonds than large stocks in order to obtain the same degree of risk (i.e., a 50/50 small-stock

and bond mix will have about the same degree of risk as a 75/25 large-stock and bond mix).

5. Beware of recency, and do not be overly impressed with asset-class returns over periods of less than two or three decades. In spite of their recent poor showing, foreign stocks and small stocks have a place in your portfolio.

6. Periodically rebalance your portfolio back to your policy allocation. This will increase your long-term return and enhance investment discipline.

5

Optimal Asset Allocations

Let's recap what we've learned so far:

1. The long-term (expected) returns and risks of many kinds of stocks and bonds are well known. Unfortunately, over periods of up to 10 or 20 years, actual returns may be significantly higher or lower than the expected return. The amount of "scatter" from the average value is known as the standard deviation (SD) and is virtually synonymous with risk.

2. Effective portfolio diversification can increase return while reducing risk. Achieving maximal benefit from effective diversification requires periodic rebalancing of portfolio composition back to the target, or "policy" composition. This is often emotionally difficult to do, as it almost always involves moving against market sentiment.

3. Whether you like it or not, you are a money manager. Asset allocation accounts for most of the difference in performance among money managers. Arriving at an effective asset allocation is both critically important and not that hard to do. Long-term success in individual security selection and market timing is difficult to impossible; fortunately, they are nearly irrelevant. The failure of market timing and active security selection will be discussed in Chapter 6.

4. Since the future cannot be predicted, it is impossible to specify in advance what the best asset allocation will be. Rather, our job is to find an allocation that will do reasonably well under a wide range of circumstances.

5. Sticking by your target asset allocation through thick and thin is much more important than picking the right asset allocation.

The Calculation of Optimal Allocations

First of all, let's be clear about what we mean when we say "optimal allocations." We can actually be talking about one of three allocations: future, hypothetical, or historical. You cannot know *future optimal portfolio composition* any more than you can sprout wings and fly, play point guard for the Lakers, or win the Miss America pageant. Anybody who tells you that they know the optimal future allocation belongs in Sing-Sing or Bellevue. (And were you actually able to do this, you sure-as-shootin' wouldn't need this book. You would know the future returns of all asset classes, and you wouldn't need asset allocation. What you would in fact need is a competent pilot for your Gulfstream V to get you back and forth between your villas in Davos, Palm Springs, Jackson Hole, and Martha's Vineyard.)

Hypothetical optimal allocation refers to the process of postulating a set of returns, SDs, and correlations and then calculating the optimal allocations for these inputs.

Historical optimal allocation, what was optimal in the past, can be calculated. This is an interesting exercise, and one that we shall shortly engage in, but it is a very poor way to determine *future* allocations.

We've already hinted at one method for calculating historical optimal allocations. Recall the portfolio "clouds" in Figures 4-9 and 4-10. The portfolios at the upper left edge of the cloud lay close to the efficient frontier and are very close to being optimal. It is not that difficult to spreadsheet the historical returns and fiddle with your allocations until you are no longer able to improve portfolio return versus risk. In fact, most spreadsheets contain an optimizer tool that will allow you to determine the portfolios which will give you the most (or even least!) return at a given SD level, or the least SD at a given level of return. This is a sort of "poor man's optimizer." However, both of these methods are quite slow and cumbersome and are not appropriate for the serious student of portfolio theory. For one thing, it is an enormous amount of work to do "what if" analyses of what happens with variations of an asset's return or SD, and almost impossible to change its correlation with other assets.

There is a much faster and easier way to optimize portfolios—mean-variance analysis, devised several decades ago by Harry Markowitz (and for which he earned a Nobel Prize). A software application which uses this method is called a *mean-variance optimizer* (MVO). An MVO will rapidly compute optimal portfolio compositions from three sets of data. These are:

1. The return for each asset
2. The standard deviation of each asset
3. The correlations among all the assets

Until very recently, MVOs were quite expensive and the input data even more so. Because of this, I spent a fair amount of effort describing spreadsheet techniques in this book's previous versions. Fortunately, this is no longer necessary. MVOs are now available for under $100, and the data has become much easier to obtain as well. See Appendix A for product and vendor information.

MVO's one disadvantage is that it does not take rebalancing into account, as it is a so-called single-period technique, and rebalancing is a multiple-period phenomenon. However, optimal portfolios are the same whether or not they are rebalanced. Further, it is relatively easy to adjust for rebalancing once the efficient frontier has been calculated.

As an example, let's consider the seven assets for the 1970–1996 period used in Figure 4-10, plus long bonds and T-bills. The complete MVO inputs for this time period are listed in Table 5-1.

The first two columns are the annualized returns and standard deviations. The adjacent columns show the correlations between the annual returns of each asset for the 27 annual-return periods.

These inputs are fed into the optimizer, in this case MVOPlus, produced by Efficient Solutions. Like all Markowitz optimizers, this program utilizes the so-called critical-line technique to produce a series of "corner portfolios," which define the composition of the efficient frontier for this set of input data. Let's take a look at the output, shown in Table 5-2. Figure 5-1 shows the actual graphical output from MVOPlus.

Corner 1 is the minimum-variance portfolio; it is the one with the least risk. Notice that it consists of 92.5% T-bills, with the other 7.5% consisting of assets that we would generally consider quite risky. Most of the portfolios in the risk range which most of us would consider reasonable, live between corners 7 and 8. Portfolios 1 through 6 consist almost entirely of short bonds, and above portfolio

Table 5-1. Optimizer Inputs for 1970–1996

	Return (%)	SD (%)	S&P	SM	EUR	PR	JAP	PM	20Y	5Y	TB
S&P	12.27	15.85	1.00								
SM	14.15	22.93	0.71	1.00							
EUR	13.05	20.95	0.63	0.42	1.00						
PR	12.26	30.84	0.50	0.51	0.53	1.00					
JAP	14.54	33.68	0.19	0.13	0.42	0.52	1.00				
PM	13.70	42.99	−0.13	−0.09	−0.02	0.35	0.09	1.00			
20Y	9.27	11.89	0.46	0.21	0.35	−0.04	0.06	−0.15	1.00		
5Y	9.28	6.86	0.38	0.14	0.20	−0.09	−0.06	−0.09	0.92	1.00	
TB	6.88	2.67	−0.08	0.00	−0.19	−0.19	−0.20	0.17	−0.03	−0.22	1.00

Key: S&P = S&P 500; SM = U.S. small stocks (CRSP 9-10 Decile); EUR = MSCI-European stocks; Pacific Rim MSCI, i.e.; PR = Pacific Rim Stocks (MSCI—excluding Japan); JAP = Japanese stocks (MSCI-Japan); PM = precious metals stocks (Morningstar Objective Category); 20Y = 20-year Treasury bond; 5Y = 5-year Treasury note; TB = 30-day Treasury bill.

Table 5-2. Corner Portfolios 1970–1996

	1	2	3	4	5	6	7	8	9	10
S&P										
SM								43.95%	45.75%	23.74%
EUR	0.29%	0.43%	0.75%	0.93%	0.96%	3.35%	15.39%	8.25%		
PR	1.76%	1.81%	1.83%	2.05%	2.04%	1.65%	0.16%			
JAP	1.24%	1.35%	1.67%	2.07%	2.11%	3.82%	10.45%	23.84%	28.03%	38.66%
PM					0.04%	1.87%	9.48%	23.96%	26.22%	37.60%
20Y	4.23%	4.45%								
5Y			8.56%	11.47%	11.74%	18.73%	64.52%			
TB	92.49%	91.95%	87.20%	83.47%	83.09%	70.58%				
Return	7.35%	7.38%	7.54%	7.70%	7.72%	8.52%	12.35%	16.61%	16.83%	17.07%
SD	2.44%	2.44%	2.46%	2.50%	2.51%	3.02%	7.80%	17.68%	18.45%	21.84%

Key: S&F = S&P 500; SM = U.S. small stocks (CRSP 9-10 Decile); EUR = MSCI-European stocks; Pacific Fim MSCI, i.e.; PR = Pacific Rim Stocks (MSCI—excluding Japan); JAP = Japanese stocks (MSCI-Japan); PM = precious metals stocks (Morningstar Objective Category); 20Y = 20-year Treasury bond; 5Y = 5-year Treasury note; TB = 30-day Treasury bill.

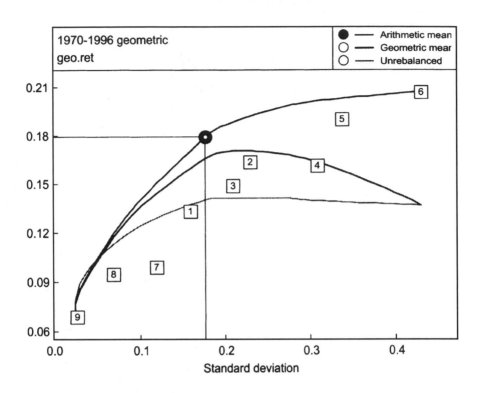

Figure 5-1. Optimizer output, MVOPlus.

Math Details:

MVOPlus has the unique ability to identify the portfolio with the maximum annualized (geometric) return, whereas all other commercially available optimizers will identify the asset with the highest arithmetic return as the last portfolio, which is not the one with the highest geometric return. This is because the difference between the arithmetic and geometric returns is approximately half its variance, or $(SD)^2/2$, and is called variance drag. As we move toward the right on the return-versus-risk plot, variance drag increases to the point where geometric return begins to fall. Remember, you "eat" geometric annualized return, not arithmetic return.

0, the portfolios become very risky. Portfolio 10 is the maximum-return portfolio.

You are not limited to the corner portfolios, of course. If you decide that halfway between portfolios 7 and 8 is where you want to be, then you simply average the compositions of the two portfolios for each asset.

Look at portfolio 7 for a moment. It is about one-third stock and two-thirds five-year Treasuries. So far, so good. But look at the equity composition—almost entirely U.S. small, Japanese, and precious metals stocks. This is not a portfolio that any rational person would own. It is no accident that these are the three assets with the highest returns for the 1970–1996 period. We've just run into optimization's fatal weakness: it is overly fond of assets with a recent history of high returns. In fact, with a bit of practice, it is possible to get the optimizer to spit out almost any portfolio you want. Change the return inputs of most assets by a few percent in either direction and that asset will either dominate the portfolio or completely disappear from it. Do you think that you can predict the future returns of all the major asset classes in your portfolio? If you can, then you are very talented indeed. Hence, the two fundamental laws of optimizers:

- An optimizer will heavily favor those assets with high historical or assumed returns.

- If you can predict the optimizer inputs well enough to come close to the future efficient frontier, then you don't need an optimizer in the first place.

The dangers of blindly feeding historical returns, SDs, and correlations into an optimizer should already be apparent from the above example. Asset returns have a tendency to "mean revert" over long time periods; an asset with stellar returns over the past 10 years is more likely than not to have below-average returns in the subsequent 10 years. Some wags have referred to optimizers as "error maximizers" for just this reason.

In order to better understand the pitfalls of optimization, let's take a look at what actually happens when one uncritically feeds historical data into an optimizer. Let's divide 1970–1998 into five-year periods with a final four-year period. Next, we'll optimize each five-year period, and see how the optimal all-stock allocation does in the subsequent five-year period compared to a "coward's portfolio" consisting of equal parts of all six stock assets (U.S. large cap, U.S. small cap, European, Pacific Rim, Japanese, and precious metals).

We start in 1970–1974. For this period, the optimal return is produced by an allocation of 99.8% precious metals and 0.2% Japan, producing 29.97% annualized. Carrying that allocation forward to 1975–1979 produced a return of 14.71% versus 25.38% for the coward's portfolio.

For 1975–1979, the optimal allocation was 100% U.S. small stocks, with a return of 39.81% annualized. This allocation actually did pretty well going forward to 1980–1984, with a return of 21.59% versus 14.75% for the coward's portfolio.

For 1980–1984, the optimal allocation was 73% U.S. small and 27% precious metals with a return of 21.94%. Going forward to 1985–1989 this allocation returned 11.83% versus 24.14% for the cowards.

For 1985–1989, the best allocation was 100% Japanese stocks, producing an astonishing return of 40.24% annualized. The next five years? *Negative* 3.5% annualized versus to plus 7.54% for the coward's portfolio.

Again, it's useful to take a short jaunt in the "wayback machine" to the late 1980s. A few square miles of Tokyo real estate were worth more than all of California, and shortly we were all going to be speaking Japanese. "The Nikkei too expensive at 100 times earnings? Westerners just don't understand how to value equity on the Tokyo markets."

And finally, for 1990–1994 the best strategy was 100% Pacific Rim, returning 15.27% annualized. For the next four years (1995–1998) this strategy returned *negative* 3.22% versus plus 6.61% for the coward's. And once again, in 1994 "everybody knew" that the Asian Tigers would attain an American standard of living within the decade.

Over the whole 1975–1998 period the above five-year optimization strategy would have returned 8.40% annualized, which is worse than any of the individual stock assets, and much worse than the 15.79% returned annually for the coward's portfolio.

What you are in effect doing by optimizing historical returns is accepting current conventional wisdom. This is not a coincidence. Markets that have experienced abnormally high returns have usually undergone a substantial increase in price as a multiple of earnings, and this is almost always the result of increasing optimism surrounding that asset.

Where do we stand with our optimizer? In the words of a former president, we are in "deep doo-doo." We can't predict returns, SDs, and correlations accurately enough. If we could, we wouldn't need the optimizer in the first place. And optimizing raw historical returns is a one-way ticket to the poor house.

So, forget about getting the answer from a magic black box. We'll have to look elsewhere for a coherent allocation strategy.

More Bad News

A well-diversified portfolio is not a free lunch. It does not come anywhere near eliminating risk; economic catastrophes do not respect national borders. The events of 1929–1932 and 1973–1974 involved all markets, and the damage varied only in degree among national markets. Markowitz mean-variance analysis tells us that if one asset has an SD of 20%, then two completely uncorrelated assets (zero correlation) will have an SD of 14.1%, and four mutually uncorrelated assets, an SD of 10%. In practical terms it is nearly impossible to find three mutually uncorrelated assets. Consequently, we cannot hope for a risk reduction of more than about one-quarter to one-third from diversification.

Worse, the correlation coefficients calculated between assets somewhat overstate the diversification benefit because the correlation of below-average returns turns out to be higher than for above-average returns. In other words, the "negative semicorrelations" are greater than the "positive semicorrelations." Translated into plain English this means that the actual correlation of asset returns in severe bear markets is higher than the "raw" correlation coefficient would suggest. The reduction in SD afforded by diversification often is lost in severe bear markets. Academician Bruno Solnik states simply, "Diversification fails us just when we need it most." This was well seen on October 19, 1987 and in the fall of 1990 when all of the world's stock indexes suffered significant losses, in spite of their low correlations in more normal times. This is why simple portfolio backtesting is a valuable supplement to MVO; one can actually see how well a proposed portfolio responded in an actual bear market.

A major argument against international diversification is that of sovereign risk—the possibility that one's assets will be expropriated by a foreign government or be lost in a war. Consider that before the Second World War two of the world's major capital markets were Germany and Egypt; one was destroyed in the war and the other nationalized after it. Latin American nations have been defaulting on their debt with near clocklike regularity for the past century. The perils of long-term international investing should not be understated, but it is important to understand the mathematical nature of long-term risk. Let us assume that at some point during a 70-year investment horizon one-half of our capital suddenly and irretrievably disappears. This lowers our long-term return by only 1.0%. Further, consider that while Japanese and German capital disappeared at the beginning of the Second World War, spectacular returns were earned in these markets in the four decades following 1945.

Others argue that because of the globalization of our economy, international diversification has lost its value. No one can doubt that our economic life is becoming increasingly globalized. The events in foreign capital markets seem to exert an instantaneous effect on our own, leading many to predict that the market returns of nations will become increasingly correlated and that the benefits of international diversification will disappear. This argument is so prevalent that it has acquired an aura of fact. Fortunately for the investor, the data indicate otherwise. For example, there is good data for the returns of U.K. and U.S. markets dating from 1919. The 1919–1994 period can be broken down into four periods of 19 years each, and correlations for annual returns can be also calculated for each period:

Period	1919–1937	1938–1956	1957–1975	1976–1994
Correlation	.66	.26	.74	.18

While the correlation between the U.S. and U.K. markets can be seen to vary widely, there is no pattern of increasing correlation; the lowest correlation is for the last period.

Similarly, it is possible to follow correlations for many individual national market returns for the 1969–1998 period. In general, there is no pattern of increasing correlation. The one exception is the increasing correlations among European markets over the past two decades.

Figure 5-2 is a plot of the correlation coefficient for the S&P 500/EAFE pair for monthly returns (three-year rolling periods) for 1969 to 1998. The correlation is seen to vary widely during this period, but there is certainly no clear-cut increase in this value over time. (There does seem to have been a rise in the correlation over the past two years or so. This was probably caused by the Asian-flu-related volatility of 1997–1998.) There is little evidence to support the notion of an increasing international market correlation resulting from a globalizing economy.

Probably of greater importance than the risk reduction derived from diversification is the "rebalancing bonus," the extra return produced by rigorous rebalancing. The benefit derived from rebalancing is not only pecuniary, but also psychological. By getting into the habit of profiting by moving in the direction opposite the market's, the investor gains both a healthy self-reliance and a scorn for market sentiment. This distrust of sentiment and "expert opinion" is one of an investor's most useful tools.

Yet another psychological benefit of a diversified portfolio results from its limited exposure to any one market segment: you are never

Figure 5-2. S&P 500/EAFE correlations, 1969–1998.

"betting the farm" on one asset. If only 5% or 10% of your portfolio is invested in emerging markets stocks, then the inevitable 30% or 50% loss occasionally seen in this area will not hurt too much; it is highly likely that gains in other areas will make up for part or all of the loss. More importantly, your low exposure may make you eager to rebalance, thus "buying cheap."

International Diversification with Small Stocks

Further diversification benefit can be obtained through the use of international small stocks. Consider the correlation grids for large and small stock returns for 1990–1998, shown in Table 5-3. The first number is the correlation for large stocks in the asset class pair, the second for small stocks.

For example, for the Japan and U.S. pair the correlation of monthly returns for large stocks is .310 and .195 for small stocks. In fact, in each case the correlation for small stocks is less than for large stocks. This effect is particularly dramatic for U.S.-U.K. and U.S.-Continental European correlations, the three classes that make up the bulk of

Table 5-3. Correlations of Global Large and Small Stocks, 1990–1998 (Monthly Returns)

	U.S.	Japan	U.K.	Cont.	Pac. Rim	Em. mkt.
U.S.	1.0/1.0					
Japan	.310/.195	1.0/1.0				
U.K.	.567/.344	.477/.419	1.0/1.0			
Cont.	.632/.339	.493/.406	.747/.660	1.0/1.0		
Pac. Rim.	.556/.475	.357/.309	.529/.282	.547/.321	1.0/1.0	
Em. mkt.	.568/.513	.284/.155	.422/.339	.582/.400	706/.688	1.0/1.0

Key: Cont. = Continental European; U.K. = Great Britain; Pac. Rim = Pacific Rim nations; Em. Mkt. = Emerging Markets nations, equally weighted portfolios.

SOURCE: Dimensional Fund Advisors.

most global portfolios. In spite of the fact that small stock indexes of *individual nations* are considerably more volatile than their larger cousins, a portfolio of global small stocks is only marginally more volatile than a similar portfolio of foreign and domestic large stocks. For example, the SD of the Dimensional Fund Advisors' global large company index for 1990–1998 was 13.46%, versus 14.37% for the global small company index.

The real risk of small stocks is their tracking error—the propensity to have returns which can be considerably lower, as well as considerably higher, than large stocks. In other words, diversification into this area works whether we want it to or not. This has been particularly painful over the past decade, as large-company stocks have outperformed small-company stocks around the globe, in spite of small stocks' higher long-term returns.

Rational investors deal with the large-versus-small dilemma in the same way as they deal with the foreign-versus-domestic problem. First and foremost, guard against recency—do not be overly impressed with the last decade's triumph of domestic over foreign, and of large over small. If anything, these phenomena make it more likely that the opposite will occur in the next decade. Second, hedge your bets with large and small stocks in the same way that Uncle Fred showed you for foreign and domestic stocks. In other words, own all "four corners" of the global equity market: large domestic, large foreign, small domestic, and small foreign.

Allocating Assets:
The Three-Step Approach

We are finally ready to allocate your assets. You must ask three questions in sequence:

1. How many different asset classes do I want to own?
2. How "conventional" a portfolio do I want?
3. How much risk do I want to take?

Asset Classes

How many different asset classes should you own? You might as well ask the meaning of life. About all one can say is "more than three." Portfolios come in many degrees of complexity, and the number of assets you employ will depend largely upon how much you tolerate dealing with this complexity. I'll make a small confession at this point; I'm an asset-class junkie—I just can't own enough of the things. I enjoy dealing with them, and if I have to manage a portfolio with 20 or 30, that's all right.

But the law of diminishing returns applies to asset classes. You get the most diversification from the first several. The next several, maybe a bit more. Beyond that you're probably just amusing yourself.

So here is the hierarchy. I'll start with level-one portfolio complexity:

The Level-One Asset Palette

U.S. large stocks (S&P 500)

U.S. small stocks (CRSP 9-10, Russell 2000, or Barra 600)

Foreign stocks (EAFE)

U.S. short-term bonds

The CRSP 9-10 is an index of small stocks, produced by the Center for Research in Security Prices, and consists of almost all stocks with market capitalization values in the bottom fifth of the New York Stock Exchange. In fact, most of its companies trade on the Nasdaq. The Russell 2000 consists of the 2000 smallest stocks in the Russell 3000 Index. Finally, the S&P 600 are 600 small companies selected by Standard & Poor's as representative of the small-cap universe.

If you don't like investing all that much, and if reading this book is the equivalent of root canal work, then these are the only four assets you really need. You can get most of the diversification of far more complex portfolios from this short list. All four of these asset classes are available as inexpensive index funds. And, as I've already said, if history is any guide a portfolio divided equally among these four assets will most likely outperform the overwhelming majority of investment professionals over the next few decades. We'll discuss later in this chapter what proportions to assign each asset.

The Level-Two Asset Palette

U.S. large stocks (S&P 500)

U.S. small stocks (CRSP 9-10, Russell 2000, or Barra 600)

Foreign large stocks

Emerging markets stocks

Foreign small stocks

REITs

U.S. short-term bonds

This palette is for the individual who is serious about diversification and wants its full benefit. You may wish to add other asset classes as well, such as precious metals stocks and international bonds.

I'm not going to list all of the possibilities that the level-three asset palette "true believer" might want to own, since it's a very long and boring one, but I will instead provide a description. Equity assets can not only be divided according to the size of company (large-versus-small) but also by value versus growth orientation. We'll talk more about value investing in Chapter 7, but suffice it to say that companies come in two value flavors—growth and value. For growth, think Microsoft, Wal-Mart, and Amazon.com. These are rapidly growing companies selling for upwards of 35 times earnings (if they have any earnings at all!), because these earnings are expected to grow rapidly. For value, think General Motors, Kmart, or J.P. Morgan. These are companies with poor growth prospects, which consequently sell more cheaply than growth stocks.

So, we now have three dimensions of stock characterization—nationality, size, and value versus-growth-orientation. You can easily divide the world up into 10 different regions, and for each you have large versus small and value versus growth. That's 40 possibilities right there. And that's not including sectors (REITs, precious metals, natural resources, utilities) or bonds for each nation. Not all of these categories are easily available in the marketplace, but a surprising number are. It is relatively easy to buy an emerging markets small-company fund, for example, if you really want one. One can go even further and buy single-country vehicles, or even individual foreign companies available on the U.S. exchanges as American Depositary Receipts (ADRs).

I don't recommend the level-three palette for anyone who doesn't truly enjoy investing and who doesn't have the time and patience to deal with its complexity.

How Unorthodox Are You?

Let's start with the level-one palette and assume that you are one of those rare individuals who can tolerate a 100% equity portfolio. Instead of the four assets listed, you only have to consider the first three. Just how do you allocate your assets between U.S. large stocks, U.S. small stocks, and foreign stocks? History tells us that small stocks have higher returns than large stocks and foreign stocks, but with greater risk. Why not simply take the "coward's way" and divide our assets equally between these three classes?

This is in fact not an unreasonable way to go and should do quite well in the long term. However, remember that whether we like it or not, U.S. large stocks are "the market." All of us, consciously or subconsciously, compare our own returns to this benchmark, usually the S&P 500.

At times, this "equal mix" also will behave very differently from the benchmark. Therefore, let's look at a portfolio which is very similar to that used by many institutional investors—60% U.S. large stocks, with 20% each U.S. small and foreign stocks (a "conventional portfolio") for the six 5-year periods starting 1969. The portfolio compositions and returns are shown in Table 5-4.

First, note that the long-term returns (last row) of all three portfolios are very similar. Also notice that the coward's portfolio underperformed the S&P 500 by 4% per year in 1969–1973 and 1989–1993, and by over 8% in the last 5-year period. (These are the boldfaced numbers in the table.) The conventional portfolio lagged the S&P by considerably less.

TABLE 5-4. Tracking Error of Various Equity Mixes, 1969–1998

	Equal mix	Conventional portfolio
S&P 500	33.33%	60%
U.S. small stocks	33.33%	20%
Foreign stocks	33.33%	20%

	S&P 500	Equal mix	Conventional portfolio
1969–1973	2.02%	**−1.99%**	−0.34%
1974–1978	4.33%	13.68%	10.01%
1979–1983	17.27%	18.84%	18.23%
1984–1988	15.39%	19.57%	17.93%
1989–1993	14.51%	**10.48%**	12.19%
1994–1998	24.06%	**15.91%**	19.21%
1969–1998	12.67%	12.50%	12.66%

While it may be true that the long-term returns of a highly diversified portfolio are the same as a more conventional portfolio, from time to time it will seriously underperform it. How much would such temporary underperformance bother you? Presumably many of you already own some small stocks and foreign stocks. How disturbed have you been by their recent laggard performance? If the answer is "very," then you should choose a portfolio more heavily weighted toward U.S. large stocks. On the other hand, if you can tolerate this sort of "tracking error," then a more unconventional portfolio heavily weighted toward foreign and small stocks may be appropriate.

As we move toward portfolios of greater complexity, this tracking error becomes more pronounced, and your tolerance to it becomes ever-more important. Recall from Chapter 4 that international small stocks have lagged the S&P 500 by 19% *per year* since 1990, even though their performance over the past 30 years has been outstanding. In fact, the more exotic asset classes you add to your mix, the higher your tracking error will be. Remember, that tracking error does not mean lower returns, it just means that your portfolio will behave very differently from everyone else's, and that it will often temporarily underperform everybody else's.

Risk Tolerance

The third step in the asset allocation process is by far the easiest. You have already done the heavy lifting—deciding what stock asset classes to use, and in approximately what proportion to use them. Now all you have to determine is the overall mix of stocks and bonds. In the first versions of this book, I recommended that the most aggressive investors might consider a 100% equity portfolio. This is because historically stocks have returned several percent more on an annual basis than bonds, albeit at considerably more risk. And yet, as we begin the new millennium, it seems highly likely that over the coming decades stock returns will be at best only slightly higher than bond returns. As already alluded to in Chapter 2, the S&P 500 currently yields about 1.3%, and historically earnings have only grown at a real (inflation-adjusted) rate of 2% per year (discussed in Chapter 2 and shown in Figure 2-12). Some may find it difficult to believe that real corporate earnings have grown at a long-term rate of only 2% per year, but this is in fact the case. In 1920 the Dow Jones Industrial Average earned $9.12 per share, and in 1998 it earned $378.06. This compounds out to just 4.89% per year. During the same period, the inflation rate was 2.87%. Thus, the real return—the difference between these two rates—was almost exactly 2%. (Dividends have grown even more slowly at 1.5% per year in inflation-adjusted terms.) This adds up to an expected real stock return of less than 3.5%. Now consider that Treasury bonds currently yield about 6%. With the inflation rate currently at 1.6%, this results in a real yield of 4.4%. And if you are afraid that an uptick in inflation may wipe out some of those real returns, you can purchase a Treasury Inflation Protected Security (TIPS) at a government-guaranteed 4.1% real yield. In other words, it is quite possible that over the next few decades stock returns may actually be less than bond returns.

For this reason, even the most aggressive investors may wish to hold perhaps 25% bonds, with moderately aggressive investors holding a 50/50 mix of stocks and bonds, and conservative investors in the range of 30% stocks and 70% bonds.

To reiterate, the aggressiveness of your portfolio is reflected in your overall stock and bond mix, not in the kinds of equity you hold, which should be similar at all levels of risk.

The Madonna Portfolio

Let's look at a few more examples of how this process works. Assume that you are a bold investor and have answered the three questions posed earlier in the chapter as follows:

1. Complexity: moderate (level-two palette, plus precious metals)
2. Conventionality: low. You have determined that you can tolerate a large amount of tracking error and do not mind at all if your allocation underperforms the S&P 500 for up to a decade, as long as your long-term returns are reasonable.
3. Risk tolerance: high. You have shown an ability to withstand large losses in your portfolio without flinching.

Here's what such a portfolio might look like:

- 10% S&P 500
- 10% U.S. small stocks
- 10% REITs
- 10% international large-cap stocks
- 10% international small-cap stocks
- 10% emerging markets stocks
- 10% precious metals stocks
- 30% U.S. short-term bonds

This portfolio is more or less equally divided between domestic and foreign, and small and large cap. It is extremely unconventional in this regard, and it will have returns that will be radically different from the S&P 500 in many years, in either direction. On the other hand, its long-term returns should be quite high. We hold a fair amount of bonds because the discounted dividend model tells us that stock returns going forward may not be much greater than bond returns. *This portfolio is not recommended for all but the hardiest of souls and most independent of thinkers.*

The Gap Portfolio

Let's answer the basic portfolio questions a bit differently:

1. Complexity: high. We don't mind holding more than a dozen asset classes.
2. Conventionality: high. We want adequate diversification and returns, but wish to keep tracking error to a minimum.

3. Risk tolerance: low. We really don't want to lose more than about 6% of our net worth in a given year.

The following portfolio is taken from the Dimensional Fund Advisors' (DFAs) "moderate balanced" strategy, with low-to-mid risk. This 40/60 stock/bond portfolio is available from DFA, about which more will be said in Chapter 8:

- 8% U.S. large-cap growth
- 8% U.S. large-cap value
- 4% U.S. small-cap growth
- 4% U.S. small-cap value
- 4% REIT
- 4% international large-cap value
- 2% international small-cap growth
- 2% international small-cap value
- 1.2% emerging markets large-cap growth
- 1.2% emerging markets large-cap value
- 1.6% emerging markets small-cap growth
- 15% one-year corporate bonds
- 15% two-year global bonds
- 15% five-year U.S. government bonds
- 15% five-year global bonds

First, the complexity of this portfolio should satisfy all but the most exacting portfolio buff, with no less than 15 asset classes. Secondly, it is quite conventional, with a 28/12 domestic/foreign split, and it is much heavier in large-cap than small-cap stocks. This portfolio provides adequate safety and diversification, and yet its return only rarely varies more than a half-dozen percent from a domestic 40/60 S&P 500/T-bill mix.

You now have an idea of how the allocation process works. First, decide how many different stock and bond asset classes you are willing to own. Increasing the number of asset classes you employ will improve diversification but will also increase your work load and tracking error. The Gap Portfolio gets around this problem with a heavy weighting of large and domestic stocks in its equity portion.

Second, decide just how much tracking error you can tolerate. If you are unable to tolerate much tracking error, keep your proportion of foreign and small-cap stocks low.

And last, adjust your stock-versus-bond mix according to how much risk you can tolerate, ranging from a maximum of 75% stock for the most aggressive investors down to 25% for the least aggressive.

Up to this point our journey through portfolio analysis has been fairly academic—we have not yet "gotten our fingers dirty" with real investments. In Chapters 6 and 7 we shall examine the nuances of how real markets actually work, and in Chapter 8 we shall explore the nuts and bolts of implementing our asset allocation plan.

Summary

1. It is impossible to forecast future optimal portfolios by any technique.

2. Over the long term, a widely diversified global portfolio of small- and large-company stocks should have favorable return-versus risk-characteristics.

3. Your precise asset allocation will depend on three factors: your tolerance to S&P 500 tracking error, the number of assets you wish to own, and your tolerance to risk.

6

Market Efficiency

There are two kinds of investors, be they large or small: those who don't know where the market is headed, and those who don't know that they don't know. This pertains to any market, be it stocks, bonds, Louis XIV chairs, or pork bellies. Then again, there is actually a third type of investor—the investment professional, who indeed knows that he or she doesn't know, but whose livelihood depends upon appearing to know.

It seems intuitively obvious that stock selection should be a skill like any other. With enough intelligence, training, experience, and effort, one should be able to beat the market.

However, the primary strength of Western culture is its reliance on the scientific method. The short version of which is that any rational belief should be *falsifiable*—that is to say, testable. Consider baseball hitters. You say that there is such a thing as "hitting skill"? A trivial thing to ask, of course, but still easy to test.

The batting analogy is useful because it forces us to think about the statistical nature of skill. Probably the best way to define it is in terms of *persistence* of performance. Let's say that the mean batting average among baseball players is .260. Now let's look at last year's .300 hitters. Were there no such thing as batting skill, then their performance this year would be merely average—in other words, .260. Of course, one year's .300 hitters *as a group* always do well above average the following year by such a wide margin as to remove all doubt that their performance is due to skill, and not chance. Interestingly, when exposed to the harsh light of statistical analysis, more than a few sports beliefs do fail to pass muster. One of these is the "hot hand" phenomenon in basketball. Feeding the ball to the shooter on a "hot streak" is a time-honored court strategy. And yet, a player who has recently hit a higher percentage of goals than his usual is no more likely than usual to do so going forward. That is, such performance does not *persist*. This highlights a human foible that has great import in finance—our tendency to see patterns where there are in fact none.

And yet, it was not until 30 years ago that researchers began to apply the same techniques to money managers. It turns out that for all practical purposes there is no such thing as stock-picking skill. The first to document this was Michael Jensen, who, in a landmark paper published in 1968 in the *Journal of Finance*, looked at mutual fund performance for the 20 years from 1945 to 1964 and found no evidence of persistence of fund performance. Last year's hot manager, on the average, will be simply mediocre next year. Since then, dozens of careful analyses of money manager performance have been done, and the results are eye-opening. Many studies show a small amount of persistence, but the effect is always so tiny that after you pay fund expenses, you still come out behind the market performance, on average. Furthermore, the persistence is usually over relatively brief periods (a year or less) and not over the longer term.

Let's take a look at some of the data. A study done by Dimensional Fund Advisors, an institutional investment firm in Santa Monica, CA, looked at fund performance for the period January 1970 to June 1998. They examined the top 30 diversified mutual funds for sequential five-year periods and then subsequent performance. The results are tabulated in Table 6-1. In each example, the top funds for the first period underperformed the S&P 500 in the subsequent period and in two of the five examples actually underperformed their peers as well.

Does this look like the performance of highly skilled money managers? No. We are looking at the proverbial bunch of chimpanzees throwing darts at the stock page. Their "success" or "failure" is a purely random affair. The most successful managers wind up being interviewed in *Money, The New York Times*, and by Uncle Lou. Their assets under management balloon, and their shareholders' admiration is vindicated by the media attention.

However, time passes, and the laws of chance eventually catch up with these folks. Hundreds of thousands of investors find that the handsome prince managing their funds turned out to be just another hairy simian. In fact, with the particularly perverse logic of fund

Math Details: How to Statistically Test for Skill

A detailed explanation of how to statistically demonstrate skill is well beyond the scope of this book. However, a simple illustration is useful. Let's use the example of a .260 mean batting average, with an SD among hitters in any given year of .020. In other words, a .300 average places the hitter 2 SDs [(.300 − .260)/.020] above the mean for that single year. If a hitter averages .280 over 10 seasons, is he skilled? The "standard error" (SE) of randomly performing batters with an annual SD .020 over a 10-year period is $0.020/\sqrt{10} = .0063$. In other words, in a random world an annual SD of 20 points translates into an SD of 6.3 points over 10 years. The difference between the batter's performance and the mean is .020, and dividing that by the SE of .0063 gives a "z value" of 3.17. Since we are considering 10 years, performance, there are 9 "degrees of freedom." The z value and degrees of freedom are fed into a "t distribution function" on our spreadsheet, and out pops a p value of .011. In other words, in a "random batting" world, there is a 1.1% chance of a given batter averaging .280 over 10 seasons.

Whether or not we consider such a batter skilled also depends on whether we are observing him "in sample" or "out of sample." *In sample* means that we picked him out of a large number of batters—say, all of his teammates—after the fact. In which case he is probably *not* skilled, since it would not be unusual for 1 of 30 individuals to experience a 1.1% random event. On the other hand, if his performance measured is *out of sample*—that is, we had picked him alone among his teammates—then he probably *is* skilled, since we would have only one chance at a 1.1% occurrence in a random batting world. An only slightly more complex formulation is used to evaluate money managers. One has to be extremely careful to distinguish out-of-sample from in-sample performance. One should not be surprised if one picks out the best-performing manager out of 500 and finds that his p value is .001. However, if one identifies him ahead of time, and then his performance p value is .001 after the fact, then he probably is skilled.

Table 6-1. Subsequent Performance of Top Performing
Funds, 1970–1998

	Return 1970–1974	Return 1975–1998
Top 30 funds 1970–1974	0.78%	16.05%
All funds	−6.12%	16.38%
S&P 500	−2.35%	17.04%
	Return 1975–1979	Return 1980–1998
Top 30 funds 1975–1979	35.70%	15.78%
All funds	20.44%	15.28%
S&P 500	14.76%	17.67%
	Return 1980–1984	Return 1985–1998
Top 30 funds 1980–1984	22.51%	16.01%
All funds	14.83%	15.59%
S&P 500	14.76%	18.76%
	Return 1985–1989	Return 1990–1998
Top 30 funds 1985–1989	22.08%	16.24%
All funds	16.40%	15.28%
S&P 500	20.41%	17.81%
	Return 1990–1994	Return 1995–1998
Top 30 funds 1990–1994	18.94%	21.28%
All funds	9.39%	24.60%
S&P 500	8.69%	32.18%

SOURCE: DFA/Micropal/Standard and Poor's.

flows, very few investors actually obtain the spectacular early returns
of the "top" funds. Worst of all, large asset inflows tend to depress
future returns because of so-called market impact costs, which will
be described later in this chapter. These early high returns inevitably
attract large numbers of investors, who wind up with merely average
performance, if they are lucky.

From Alpha Man to Apeman

One of the best illustrations of how this reversal can occur is
provided by Robert Sanborn, who ran Oakmark Fund. Mr. Sanborn
is an undisputed superstar manager. From inception in 1991 to year-
end 1998 Oakmark's annualized return was 24.91% versus 19.56% for

the S&P 500. In 1992 it beat the benchmark by an astonishing 41.28%. By any statistical criteria Mr. Sanborn's performance could not have been due to chance.

However, a different story emerges when we examine the fund's performance and assets by individual year. The first row tracks the performance of Oakmark Fund relative to the S&P 500, the second row tracks the fund's assets:

	1992	1993	1994	1995	1996	1997	1998
Return ±S&P 500	41.30%	20.40%	2.00%	−3.10%	−6.70%	−0.80%	−24.90%
Assets ($ millions)	328	1214	1626	3301	4194	7301	7667

What we see is the all-too-familiar pattern of fund investors chasing performance, with more and more investors getting lower and lower returns. In fact, if we "dollar weight" the fund's returns, we find that because most investors hopped on the bandwagon after the best returns had occurred, the average investor in this fund underperformed the S&P 500 by 7.55% annually.

In defense of Mr. Sanborn, it is fair to point out that S&P 500 tracking error is not a reasonable measure over the past few years for a value manager's performance. One can get around this by calculating the fund's *alpha*, which refers to the excess return added by a manager after taking into account such factors as market exposure, median company size, and value orientation. This is done with a technique (available in most spreadsheet packages) known as *regression analysis*, in which the monthly or quarterly returns for the manager in question are laid alongside the returns of benchmarks for various market factors or sectors. The manager's returns are "fitted" to the returns of the other factors, resulting in a custom-made benchmark for that manager. The alpha is the difference between the fund's performance and that of the regression-determined benchmark and a measure of how well the manager has performed. It is expressed the same way as return, in percent per year, and can be positive or negative. For example, if a manager has an alpha of −4% per year this means that the manager has underperformed the regression-determined benchmark by 4%

annually. Oakmark's alpha for the first 29 months is truly spectacular, and quite statistically significant, with a p value of .0004. This means that there was less than a 1-in-2000 possibility that the fund's superb performance in the first 29 months could have been due to chance. Unfortunately, its performance in the last 29-month period was equally impressive, but in the wrong direction.

My interpretation of the above data is that Mr. Sanborn is modestly skilled. "Modestly skilled" is not at all derogatory in this context, since 99% of fund managers demonstrate no evidence of skill whatsoever. However, unfortunately even these skills were overwhelmed by the "impact-cost drag" (to be discussed in the next section) of managing billions of dollars of new assets, chasing up stock prices and lowering ultimate returns.

The take-home message here is clear. It's human nature to find patterns where there are none and to find skill where luck is a more likely explanation (particularly if you're the lucky manager). But successful or lucky actively managed funds sow the seeds of their own destruction. Avoid them.

Why Fund Managers Do So Poorly

Mutual fund manager performance does not persist and the return of stock picking is zero. This is as it should be, of course. These folks *are* the market, and there is no way that they can all perform above the mean. Wall Street, unfortunately, is not Lake Wobegon, where all the children are above average.

So the bad news is that the process of mutual fund selection gives essentially random results. However, the *really* bad news is that actively managed funds are so expensive. Funds, of course, incur costs. Sadly, even the best-informed fund investors are usually unaware of just how high these costs really are.

Most investors think that the fund's *expense ratio* (ER), listed in the prospectus and annual reports, is their true cost of fund ownership. Wrong. There are actually three more layers of expenses beyond the ER, which merely comprises the fund's advisory fees (what the managers get paid) and administrative expenses. The next layer of fees are the commissions paid on transactions. These are not included in the ER, but since 1996 the SEC has required that they be reported to shareholders. However, they are presented in such an obscure manner that, unless you have an accounting degree, it is almost impossible to calculate how much return is lost as a proportion of fund assets.

The second extra layer is the bid-ask spread of stocks bought and sold. A stock is always bought at a slightly higher price than it is sold, to provide the market maker with a profit. This "spread" is about 0.4% for the largest, most liquid, companies and increases with decreasing company size. For the smallest stocks it may be as large as 10%. It is in the range of 1% to 4% for foreign stocks. For example, at the market close of business on April 12, 2000, Microsoft was quoted at a bid (the price at which an investor could sell the stock) of $80.125 and an ask (the price at which an investor could buy the stock) of $80.25. The difference—one-eighth of a dollar—is the spread. Because Microsoft is one of the most actively traded stocks in the world, this represents just 0.15% of the price. At the other end of the spectrum, on the same day Officeland, a tiny company dealing in used copying machines, traded at $0.65/$0.70 of bid to ask, a spread of 7.7%.

The last layer of extra expense—so-called market-impact costs—is the most difficult to estimate. Impact costs arise when large blocks of stock are bought and sold. Imagine that you own half the shares of a small publicly traded company worth $20 million. Let's further imagine that you have gotten yourself into a jam, need cash, and must quickly sell all of those shares. The selling pressure caused by your actions will drastically reduce the stock's price, and the last shares sold will fetch considerably less than the first shares sold. The reverse would occur if an investor decided that he or she wanted to quickly acquire a large block of your company.

Impact costs are not a problem for small investors buying shares of individual companies, but they are a real headache for large mutual funds. Obviously, the magnitude of impact costs depends on the size of the fund, the size of the company, and the total amount transacted. As a first approximation, assume that it is equal to the spread.

The Four Layers of Mutual Fund Costs

- Expense ratio
- Commissions
- Bid-ask spread
- Market-impact costs

Table 6-2. Active Fund Expenses

	Large cap	Small cap and foreign	Emerging markets
Expense ratio	1.30%	1.60%	2.00%
Commissions	0.30%	0.50%	1.00%
Bid-ask spread	0.30%	1.00%	3.00%
Impact costs	0.30%	1.00%	3.00%
Total	2.20%	4.10%	9.00%

Taken together, these four layers of expenses are smallest for large-cap funds, intermediate for small-cap and foreign funds, and greatest for emerging-markets funds. They are tabulated in Table 6-2.

Recall that the return of large stocks for 1926–1998 was 11.22% per year. It should be painfully obvious that this is not the return that you, the mutual fund investor, would actually receive. You must subtract out of that return the fund's total investment expense.

Now the full magnitude of the problem becomes clear. The bottom row of Table 6-2 shows the real costs of owning an actively managed fund. In fairness, this does overstate things a bit. Money spent on research and analysis is not a total loss. Such research does seem to increase returns, but almost always by an amount less than that spent. How much of the first "expense ratio" line is spent on research? Figure about a half, if you're lucky. So if the long-term return of equity in general is about 11%, then active management will lose you about 1.5% in a large-cap fund, 3.3% in a foreign or small-cap fund, and 8% in an emerging-markets fund, leaving you with 9.5%, 7.7%, and 3%, respectively. Not an appetizing prospect. The mutual fund business has benefited greatly by the high returns of recent years, which have served to mask the staggering costs in most areas. One exception to this has been in the emerging markets, where the combination of low asset-class returns and high expenses has resulted in a mass exodus of investors.

A Case Study: The January Effect

One of the great ironies of investing is that the universal availability of financial information is in fact the reason behind the failure of security analysis. Before the Securities Act of 1933 mandated periodic public disclosure of corporate performance, even the most basic financial information about a company was usually a closely guarded secret. When Benjamin Graham wrote the first edition of *Security Analysis*, the simple act of ascertaining a company's earnings or revenues was often a matter of spending a day or two on a train, then sweet-talking the information out of a secretary while being careful to avoid her boss's watchful eye. Such efforts were often well-rewarded.

In the information age, every aspect of a company's finances is immediately available to anyone with a computer and modem. And since everyone has access to this data, it is immediately discounted into the security's price, so there is no further profit from acting on it.

An excellent example of how the process works is provided by the "January effect" (JE). The JE is explained as follows:

- Small-company stocks, because of their higher risks, have a higher return than large-company stocks.

- For many decades almost all of this excess return occurred in January.

Table 6-3 shows that the January excess return is actually larger than the excess return for the entire year for the smallest stocks, as measured by Ibbotson Associates. Ibbotson divides domestic stocks into deciles by New York Stock Exchange sizes and then measures the 1926–1994 excess return over the largest (first) decile.

The precise reason for the concentration of small-stock excess return in January is unknown, but there is no shortage of candidates.

Table 6-3. Return in Excess of First Decile

Decile	January	Whole year
2	1.10%	1.49%
3	1.47%	2.04%
4	1.76%	2.33%
5	2.84%	3.14%
6	3.29%	3.06%
7	3.86%	3.24%
8	5.20%	3.86%
9	6.86%	4.54%
10	10.28%	7.82%

SOURCE: *Stocks, Bonds, Bills, and Inflation*, 1995 Yearbook, Ibbotson.

End-of-year tax-loss selling is my favorite, but there are no easy answers. Entire how-to books have been devoted to the "incredible January effect," and it's also a perennial late-year topic for material-starved financial writers.

Unfortunately, there are two fundamental problems with the JE. First, its magnitude is roughly equivalent to the bid-ask spread for each decile. For example, look at the January excess return of 10.28% for the smallest (decile 10) stocks. In order to realize that excess return, you would have had to buy each stock on December 31 and have sold it on January 31. But since the ask (buying) price for these smallest stocks is also about 10% above the bid (selling) price, you would not have made an actual profit. In other words, the simple act of buying and selling small stocks eliminates the benefit. So if you want to realize the January effect, you have to hold small stocks for many years.

The second problem is that the JE no longer exists. Figure 6-1 shows the 10-year rolling average of the small-cap premium, calculated as the difference between the January return of the CRSP 9-10 Index and the S&P 500. As can be seen, the effect has faded into insignificance. This is one of the reasons why profitable strategies, if they exist at all, do not last for very long. As soon as they are discovered, they are acted upon by the investment community, bidding up the price of the relevant assets, thus eliminating their excess return.

The Indexing Solution

Money manager, writer, and financial elder statesman Charles Ellis observed three decades ago with growing alarm the first data demonstrating a lack of money manager skill. He thought to himself, "I've seen this somewhere else." An avid tennis player, he realized that for most amateur participants winning or losing was less a matter of skill than simply playing conservatively and avoiding mistakes. He wrote a famous article, appearing in the 1972 *Financial Analysts Journal* called "The Loser's Game," in which he compared professional investing to amateur tennis. Just as the amateur tennis player who simply tries to return the ball with a minimum of fancy moves is the one who usually wins, so too does the investor who simply buys and holds a widely diversified stock portfolio. This investor is the one who

Figure 6-1. Ten-year January CRSP 9–10 decile minus S&P.

usually comes out on top. The title of the piece refers to the concept that in both amateur tennis and professional investing, success is less a matter of winning than avoiding losing. And the easiest way to lose in investing is to incur high costs by trading excessively.

The ultimate loss-avoidance strategy, then, is to simply buy and hold the entire market, i.e., to *index*. The reason should be apparent from the preceding discussion of fund costs. Since constantly analyzing and adjusting your portfolio results in high expenses and almost no excess return, why not just work at minimizing all four layers of expenses by buying and holding the market? Table 6-4 lists the four expense layers for an indexed approach to investing. The last row shows the theoretical difference in returns between the active and indexed approach.

Again, it has to be pointed out that this is a *theoretical* advantage, since at least some of the active-fund expenses are spent on research, which has been shown to be of benefit. But remember that research expenses almost never completely pay for themselves, and only a small portion of an active fund's total four-layer expense structure is spent on analysis. The basic thing to remember about research expense is that it results in turnover, which in turn increases total expense through commissions, spreads, and impact costs.

Table 6-4. Index Fund Expenses

	Large cap	Small cap and foreign	Emerging markets
Expense ratio	0.18%	0.20%	0.57%
Commissions	0.01%	0.10%	0.10%
Bid-ask spread	0.02%	0.15%	0.40%
Impact costs	0.02%	0.15%	0.40%
Total	0.23%	0.60%	1.47%
Total active fund expense	2.20%	4.10%	9.00%
Indexing Advantage	**1.97%**	**3.50%**	**7.53%**

Math Details

The average random scatter of active manager returns in any given year has about 8% of SD, but over an n year period (where n is the number of years) that scatter will be reduced by the square root of n. In other words, over a four-year period the returns scatter of active managers is reduced by half, and over 25 years by 80%. So, over a 25-year period, the random scatter (SD) of fund performance will be 8%/5 = 1.6%.

So, we see that the average active manager is flying into an annual headwind of anywhere between 1% and 8%. Since the SD, or "scatter" of annual returns for active funds is about 8% in any given year, a difference of a few percent may not be noticed. But over many years, it takes a toll, as the SD of 25-year returns is only 1.6% (see Math Details).

For large-cap funds, this means that the index-fund advantage, which has about the same 1.6% value, will result in a +1 SD performance. Meaning that the index fund should beat 84% of actively managed funds. A small or foreign index fund with a 3.2% advantage should perform 2 SDs above the norm, meaning that it should beat 97% of active funds over a 25-year period. And an emerging-markets index fund with a several-percentage-point advantage should best all of its actively managed peers.

Unfortunately, the real world is not nearly this neat, and it is worth looking at the actual data. We shall compare index-fund and active-fund performance with the Morningstar Principia database. This nifty tool is worth some discussion. Morningstar is the premier purveyor of mutual fund data for both small and institutional investors. It is best known for its print publications, available in most large public libraries, but I highly recommend the Principia software package. The guts of the program are monthly returns for 11,000 or so mutual funds, and more importantly, benchmark indexes. This allows you to calculate, display, and graph fund rankings and performance in an almost infinite variety of ways, and even to calculate correlations among funds and asset classes via their indexes. A wide variety of other information regarding valuation and fund operational data is also included. Much of my research depends on this package.

For starters, it is important to realize that we have to be careful just how we benchmark and compare our actively managed funds. The earliest persistency studies simply looked at all equity funds. This is suboptimal. It is important to compare like with like. For example, over the past several years large cap growth stocks (think McDonald's, Microsoft, Wal-Mart) have been the strongest performers. It would be unfair to compare a small-cap or foreign fund to general-equity funds, which as a group tend to have a heavy concentration of these stocks, or to the S&P 500 for the same reason. Principia employs a particularly effective approach to this problem. They divide domestic stock funds into a 3-by-3 grid of size versus value orientation. They categorize funds by company size into small, medium, and large. They also pigeonhole funds as value, growth, or "blend" (halfway between growth and value). This produces nine categories and is a good way to compare performance between funds fairly.

Let's start with the granddaddy of all index mutual funds, the Vanguard 500 Index Fund. It is no accident that sometime within the next year this should become the biggest mutual fund in the world. Over the 15-year period ending December 1998 it ranked in the 8th percentile of the Morningstar "large-cap blend" category, meaning that it beat over 92% of its peers. This is actually better than we'd expect from a fund with a 1.5% expense advantage in a category with 8% SD of annual active-manager scatter ($\sqrt{15} \times 1.5/8 = 0.73$ SD above the mean, which is about 23rd percentile). We'll come to the reason why in a minute.

Math Details: The Ultimate Benchmark

If you're really serious about benchmarking a fund, as well as look-ing for skill, you perform a three-factor regression on fund returns. Here's how it works. Developed by Ken French of MIT and Eugene Fama of University of Chicago, the regression starts with monthly returns for the broad stock market, as well as monthly return con-tributions for small-stock and value-stock exposure. You then lay the monthly returns for the fund or manager in question side by side with these three benchmark series and perform a multiple regression. This statistical technique, available on most spreadsheet packages, produces the "best fit" of the three factors to the man-ager returns series and spits out a blizzard of output numbers. The most-important of these is the residual return (the intercept of the regression), or *alpha*. The alpha is the excess return left after expo-sure to the market, size, and value have been taken into account. For most managers, it is a negative number. The output also includes the statistical significance of the alpha, telling us how likely it is the results are due to chance (a low p value suggesting skill or lack thereof, depending on whether it is positive or nega-tive). It also calculates the actual behavior of the portfolio along the small-large and value-growth axes. This methodology is now the preferred technique for measuring performance of pension fund managers and is also heavily favored in the academic community.

Vanguard also runs two other large-cap index funds, one for growth and one for value. Over the five-year period ending December 1998, the Growth Index Fund ranked in the 2nd percentile of the Morningstar large-cap growth category. The Value Index Fund ranked in the 21st percentile of its large-cap value category. Again, both of these are better than we'd calculate from the above formulation, which would predict only about 34th percentile five-year performance.

Finally, to complete the picture, let's look at small-cap indexing. The oldest small-cap index fund is the Dimensional Fund Advisors

(DFA) 9-10 Small Company Fund. Over the past 15 years, it has ranked in the 57th percentile, actually worse than average.

A superficial analysis of the above data suggests that indexing works for large-cap stocks, but not for small-cap stocks. But if we dig a little deeper, we find that this is not the case. There is a direct relationship between how well indexing works in a particular asset category and how well that asset category is doing compared to other asset classes.

Let's consider the extraordinary performance of the Vanguard Growth Index Fund, with it's 2nd percentile five-year record. It is no accident that the Barra Large Cap Growth Index, which it tracks, had the highest five-year return of any asset class—27.94% annualized— for the five-year period from 1994 to 1998. The Value Index Fund did reasonably well also, at 21st percentile for the period. Again, its tracking index, the Barra Large Cap Value Index, did reasonably well, returning 19.88% for the period.

Now, compare the 15-year 8th percentile ranking of the Vanguard 500 to the DFA 9-10 Small Company Index Fund's 57th percentile ranking. It is no coincidence that the 15-year returns of their tracking indexes were 17.91% and 9.17%, respectively. If one looks a little closer at the performance of these two index funds, one finds that there is a direct relationship between how well small stocks did vig-'a-vis large stocks and their relative rankings. For example, for the three-year period from 1992 to 1994, small stocks outperformed large stocks by 7.59% annually, and the Vanguard 500 Index Fund ranked in only the 46th percentile of its category, while the DFA 9-10 Small Company ranked in the 13th percentile of its category.

Dunn's Law

There is in fact a relationship between asset-class performance and index-fund performance, known as *Dunn's law* (after Steve Dunn, a friend with an astute eye for asset classes):

> "When an asset class does relatively well, an index fund in that class does even better."

The mechanism behind this is relatively straightforward. Let's again take the performance of the DFA 9–10 Small Company Index Fund and the Vanguard 500 Index Fund as examples. An index fund takes the full brunt of an asset class's excellent or poor performance relative to other asset classes. During the past 15 years, most actively managed small-cap funds have owned some midsize and large stocks, and this has helped their performance relative to the small-cap index. The reverse is also true of almost all actively managed large-cap funds, which frequently own stocks smaller than those in the S&P 500. This has hurt their performance relative to the S&P 500.

So, to summarize, because of the dominance of large-company stock returns over the past 15 years, large-cap indexing looks better than it actually is, and small-cap indexing looks worse than it actually is.

The same phenomenon is observed in other areas. DFA's index funds for REITs and international small companies have poor percentile rankings. This is *not* due to any lack of efficacy of indexing in these areas but rather to an artifact of the poor performance of the asset classes themselves.

The situation with international indexing is extremely interesting. Charles Schwab has the oldest diversified international index fund, and its five-year ranking for 1994–1998 is a respectable 21st percentile. If one uses the EAFE index as a proxy index fund, one comes up with an awful 10-year 90th percentile ranking, but an amazing 1st percentile 15-year ranking. The problem here is called "Japan." The EAFE until recently was overweighted in Japan, which comprised 65% of the index at the height of the Nikkei bubble in the late 1980s. During periods when Japanese equity did particularly poorly, so did foreign indexing, and vice versa. However, it is heartening to note that in spite of the fact that Japan underperformed the EAFE as a whole by more than 5% annually over the past 15 years, there is not one diversified international fund with a higher return over the same period, because of the expense advantage.

As we discussed earlier, the biggest theoretical advantage of indexing should be in the emerging-markets area. And in fact, over the past five years the DFA and Vanguard Emerging Markets Funds have ranked in the 10th and 15th percentile of their peers, respectively, in spite of the terrible returns of this asset class for the period.

A Possible Exception

One place where indexing seems to fail, even after all of the above factors are taken into consideration, is the area of small-cap growth stocks. These companies are highly entrepreneurial, rapidly growing affairs, and there are data to support the notion that resources spent on researching these companies may more than pay for itself. Another reason may be that these stocks often exhibit considerable price "momentum." A small-cap indexing strategy would of necessity sell the most rapidly appreciating stocks as they grew beyond the index's size borders, when in fact these are the companies with the highest returns going forward.

As we'll discuss further along in this chapter, small-cap growth stocks have poor long-term returns, and it is probably wise to avoid investing in this area, active or indexed.

Survivorship Bias

The deeper one delves, the worse things look for actively managed funds. Consider for a moment what happens when you open up the quarterly *New York Times* supplement and start sampling fund performance over the past 10 years. You might think that you're getting a fairly accurate picture of historical fund performance. And you'd be wrong. That is because what you're looking at is not the performance of all of the funds in existence over the past decade, but *only the ones that survived.* In other words, the very worst funds in the group got killed off (or more likely, merged with other funds), so you are looking at an overly optimistic picture of overall fund performance.

Burton Malkiel, author of *A Random Walk Down Wall Street*, has looked at this problem in some detail, and he estimates that the effect is on the order of 1.5%. In other words, the reported performance of the average fund category is about 1.5% higher than that of the true category performance. And it's almost certainly higher for some fund categories, particularly small stocks, where it may be as much as 3%. This is not a small point. I screened the Morningstar Principia database (November 1999) for domestic small-cap funds. I found 213 with a five-year track record, with an average annualized five-year return of 12.19%. The index funds in the category had only slightly higher returns (Vanguard Small Cap Fund, 13.64%; DFA 9-10 Small Company Fund 13.10%). So you might or might not be impressed with their performance. But Morningstar's database contains only surviving funds, so it's likely that the true average annualized return for the group is actually in the 9%–10% range. In which case the index funds have done very well indeed.

Do You Pay Taxes?

If the case I've presented for indexing is not powerful enough, then consider the effect of taxes. While many of us hold funds in our retirement accounts, where taxability of distributions is not an issue, most investors also own funds in taxable accounts.

While it is probably not a good idea to own actively managed funds in general, it is a truly terrible idea in taxable accounts, for two reasons. First, because of their higher turnover, actively managed funds have higher distributions of capital gains, which are taxed at your capital gains rate at both the federal and state level. An index fund allows your capital gains to grow largely undisturbed until you sell.

There is another factor to consider as well. Most actively managed funds are bought because of their superior performance. But as we've demonstrated above, this outperformance does not persist, and most small investors using active fund managers tend to turn over their mutual funds for this reason once every several years, generating more unnecessary capital gains and resultant taxes. *For the taxable investor, indexing means never having to say you're sorry.*

A caveat about small-cap indexing and taxes. Small-cap index funds (both foreign and domestic) tend to have higher turnovers than large foreign and domestic index funds. Even worse, they generate high capital gains distributions proportionate to their turnover, since the primary reason for selling a stock is a large price increase, resulting in that stock's "graduating" out of the index. For this reason, they may not be suitable for taxable investors. Fortunately, "tax managed" small-cap and large-cap index funds are now available. These strive to minimize distributions, and more will be said about them in Chapter 8.

As mutual funds have become the primary investment vehicle of small investors, they have come to manage ever more massive amounts of capital—about $5 trillion at the time of this writing. But the *real* money is managed by pension funds—about twice as much. The Investment Company Institute estimates that in 1998 only 7% of mutual fund assets were indexed, versus 34% of the pension assets of the 200 largest U.S. corporations.

It should come as no surprise that the world's biggest money managers have embraced indexing. The world of pension management is complex. There are four basic players here, and it's useful to survey the scene. The first two are the pension fund sponsors (the corporations themselves) and their employees and beneficiaries. Next are the pension fund managers. The competition for pension fund investment management slots is unbelievable. Although these managers are paid only a few basis points of money managed, 0.02% of $10 billion annually ain't chump change. Underperform the benchmark for more than a few quarters and "you're toast." Last are the *pension consultants.* Their primary function is to go out and find the "best" of these money managers for the pension sponsors.

By now, you know how this movie ends. Almost none of these managers in reality has even a drop of skill. Like our mutual fund managers, they are just one more tribe of hairy apes throwing projectiles at a stock list. Some will get lucky and attract the attention of the pension consultants, who will sell them to the sponsors. Following which the laws of probability take over and they underperform, get sacked (perhaps along with the pension consultant that found them), and the cycle starts again. This is one expensive merry-go-round—approximately 1% of $10 trillion of total pension expenses annually, or $100 billion.

On the average, these pension funds hold about a 60/40 stock/bond mix. Consulting firm Piscataqua Research found that for the period 1987–1996 only 8% of the nation's largest pension plans actually beat an indexed 60/40 mix.

So, one by one the light bulbs go on over at the pension fund sponsors, out go the stock pickers, and in many cases even the pension consultants themselves. It seems highly likely that in the next decade most pension money will be indexed. And so should yours.

Investment Newsletters

OK, so human beings cannot pick stocks. Perhaps a more fruitful approach would be to time the market and avoid losses by pulling out of stocks during the bear markets. Maybe investment newsletter writers, whose specialty this is, might help us do better. John Graham and Campbell Harvey, two finance academics, recently performed an exhaustive review of 237 newsletters. They measured the ability of these newsletters to time the market and found that less than one-quarter of the recommendations were correct, much worse than the monkey score of 50%. Even worse, there were no advisors whose calls were consistently correct, although there were many who were wrong with amazing regularity. They cited one very well known advisor whose predictions produced an astounding annualized 5.4% loss during a 13-year period when the S&P 500 produced a 15.9% gain. Astonishingly, there is even a newsletter which ranks the performance of other newsletters; its publisher believes that he can identify persistently excelling advisors. The work of Graham and Harvey suggests that in reality he is actually the judge at a coin-flipping contest. When it comes to newsletter writers, remember Malcolm Forbes' famous dictum: the only money made in newsletters is through subscriptions, not from taking the advice.

Noted author, analyst, and money manager David Dreman, in *Contrarian Market Strategy: The Psychology of Stock Market Success,* painstakingly tracked expert opinion back to 1929 and found that it underperformed the market with 77% frequency. It is a recurring theme of almost all studies of "consensus" or "expert" opinion that it underperforms the market about three-fourths of the time. Mr. Dreman argues that this is a powerful argument *against* the efficient market hypothesis: how can the markets be efficient when the experts lose with such depressing regularity?

All of this evidence falls under the rubric of what is known as *market efficiency.* A detailed discussion of the efficient market hypothesis is beyond the scope of this book, but what it means is this: it's futile to analyze the prospects for an individual stock (or the entire market) on the basis of publicly available information, since that information has already been accounted for in the price of the stock (or market). Cognoscenti frequently respond to news about a company with a weary, "It's already been discounted into the stock price." In fact, a very good argument can be made that the market more often than not overreacts to events, falling too much on bad news and rising too much on good news. The corollary of the efficient market hypothesis is that you are better off buying and holding a random selection, or as we have shown above, an index of stocks rather than attempting to analyze the market.

I am continually amazed at the amount of time the financial and mass media devote to well-regarded analysts attempting to divine the movements of the market from political and economic events. This is a fool's errand. Almost always these analysts are the employees of large brokerage houses; one would think that these organizations would tire of looking foolish on so regular a basis. (If you are not convinced of the futility of trying to predict market direction from economic conditions, then consider that the biggest money is made by buying when things look the bleakest: 1932, 1937, 1975, and 1982 were all great times to buy stocks. Then consider that the most dangerous times to buy or own stocks is when there is plenty of economic blue sky; those who bought in 1928, 1936, or 1966 were soon sorry.)

In the end, it is easy to understand why the aggregate efforts of all of the nation's professional money managers fail to best the market: They *are* the market.

Dealing with Mr. Market

There is a small town not far from where I live which has only one store. An owner of the store, who died many years ago, had a manic-depressive disorder. One week he would be in the manic phase, cheerful and expansive, and during these periods would mark up the prices of his goods. The next week he might become depressed and would mark down prices. The townspeople learned to stock up during his depressed periods and buy only what was necessary when he was manic. The financial markets are about as rational as this store owner, and the intelligent investor stocks up when prices are low and lightens up when they are high. It would be very silly indeed to mimic the moods of our store owner, and buy tomatoes simply because their price was rising. Yet this seems to be what most investors, especially professionals, do. This sort of behavior is deeply ingrained in human nature; nobody likes being left out of the party. Some readers will note the similarity of our store owner to Mr. Market from Ben Graham's *The Intelligent Investor*. If you read only one book about stocks, this should be it; my book is named in its honor.

Mr. Graham, in fact, wrote a famous article in a women's magazine many decades ago in which he made the sexist but wise recommendation that stocks should be bought in the same manner as groceries, and not perfume. Had he instead advised men to buy stocks like they buy gasoline, and not like they buy automobiles, he would have offended our tender modern sensibilities less.

The trick for the small investor, then, is to know just how much he or she is paying for those tomatoes. You know that they are a bargain at 25 cents per pound; you know you are being robbed at $3 per pound. Buying a stock or a market sector without knowing how cheap or expensive it is constitutes the pinnacle of foolishness. As we shall see in Chapter 7, determining the cheapness (or "valuation") of a market sector is quite easy.

Not Quite a Random Walk

By now I hope that I've convinced you that market movements are essentially a "random walk"—unpredictable in every regard, making stock selection and market timing an impossibility. It turns out that market movements are not totally random, and although it is nearly impossible to profit from this behavior, it still behooves the investor to be aware of market patterns. In order to do this, we have to be clear about what we mean by the term *random walk*. This means that yesterday's, last month's, or last year's market return conveys no information about future returns. Is this strictly true?

To answer this question we first have to ask how one goes about looking for nonrandom behavior. There are dozens of ways to do so, but the simplest is to look for "autocorrelations" in price changes. What we are in effect asking is, "Does the price change from the previous day, week, month, year, or decade correlate with the price change of the succeeding day, week, month, year, or decade?"

Let's take the monthly returns for the S&P 500 from January 1926 to September 1998. That's 873 months. Then create two separate series, the first with the first return eliminated, the second with the last return eliminated. What we now have are two series of 872 monthly returns, offset by one month. Thanks to the magic of modern spreadsheets, it is a simple matter to calculate a correlation coefficient of these two series. The output of this correlation of a returns series with a lagged version of itself is called an *autocorrelation*. A positive autocorrelation means that above or below average returns tend to repeat, or trend. The "momentum" of a given asset class or security is defined by a positive autocorrelation. A negative autocorrelation defines so-called mean reversion, meaning that an above-average return tends to be followed by a below-average return and vice versa. And finally, a zero autocorrelation defines a random walk.

It turns out that the autocorrelation of large stocks' monthly returns for 1926 through 1998 is .081. Not terribly impressive, but positive nonetheless, meaning that a good return this month means a slightly better than average chance of a good return next month. What are the odds that this could have happened by chance? In order to determine this, we have to calculate the standard deviation of autocorrelations for a data series of 873 random data points. The formula for this is $\sqrt{(n-1)/n}$, which for 873 is .034. Thus, the autocorrelation of .081 is more than twice the random-walk standard deviation of .034. This in turn means that the odds of this occurring with 873 random numbers is less than 1 in 100.

So, yes, U.S. security prices appear to exhibit some momentum over periods of one month.

A nice summation of the autocorrelation data for U.S. stocks is found in Campbell, Lo, and MacKinlay's (CLM) *The Econometrics of Financial Markets*. The following table summarizes their autocorrelation data for 1962 through 1984. The value-weighted (also known as the CRSP 1–10 Index) and equally weighted indexes can be very roughly thought of as large-stock and small-stock proxies, respectively.

	CRSP value-weighted (large stocks)	CRSP equally weighted (small stocks)
Daily returns	.176	.350
Weekly returns	.015	.203
Monthly returns	.043	.171

Key: CRSP = Center for Research in Security Prices.

This data pretty conclusively demonstrates momentum effects of high statistical significance for an index of large stocks from day to day, but not for longer periods. An index of small stocks does demonstrate momentum over days, weeks, and months. (I wouldn't get too excited over the .350 autocorrelation for small stocks for daily periods. Remember that many of these securities do not trade every day, so that a big market move up or down one day will be followed by appropriate moves in ensuing days in the stocks that did not trade.)

It is rather amazing that when CLM looked for momentum in individual stocks, none was found. In other words, the generations of investors who have been gazing at stock price charts likely have been wasting their time, but the recent phenomenon of charting mutual fund prices may have some validity. CLM explain this apparent paradox by noting that there are highly significant "cross autocorrelations" between large and small stocks, meaning a rise or fall in large stocks is usually followed by a rise or fall in small stocks.

What It All Means

OK, so movements are not completely random. How does this data affect the average investor? Only at the margins. Lest we get too carried away, the most impressive autocorrelations we've encountered are in the .2 range. That means that no more than 4% (.2 squared, or R-squared) of tomorrow's price change can be explained by today's. That doesn't buy a lot of yachts. For the taxable investor, this stuff is totally irrelevant—whatever advantage there is to this technique is obliterated by the capital gains capture from buying and selling with the high frequency necessitated by momentum techniques.

Certainly, however, these effects cannot be ignored. For the tax-sheltered asset allocator, the message is loud and clear: Do not rebalance too frequently.

If asset-class prices have a tendency to trend over relatively long periods (say months, or even one to two years) then rebalancing over relatively short periods will not be favorable. This is a somewhat tricky concept. Asset variance (which is the square of the standard deviation) is one of the main engines of rebalancing benefit. If an asset has momentum, then the annualized variances will be greater over long periods than over short periods—this is in fact a good way to test for momentum.

Think about the Japanese and U.S. markets. Both have exhibited pretty impressive momentum (in opposite directions) since 1989. Obviously, rebalancing as little as possible from the U.S. to Japan would have been more advantageous than doing it frequently.

Yet another way of thinking about this is the following paradigm— rebalance only over time periods where the average autocorrelation of your assets is zero or less. In practical terms, this means rebalancing no more than once per year.

Yin, Yang

Rather than being polar opposites, momentum investing and fixed-asset allocation with contrarian rebalancing are simply two sides of the same coin. Momentum in foreign and domestic equity asset classes exists, resulting in periodic asset overvaluation and undervaluation. Eventually long-term mean reversion occurs to correct these excesses.

Over 2 decades ago, Eugene Fama made a powerful case that security price changes could not be predicted, and Burton Malkiel introduced the words "random walk" into the popular investing lexicon. Unfortunately, in a truly random-walk world, there is no advantage to portfolio rebalancing. If you rebalance, you profit only when the frogs in your portfolio turn into princes, and vice versa.

In the real world, fortunately, there are subtle departures in random-walk behavior that the asset allocator-investor can exploit. Writer and money manager Ken Fisher calls this change in asset desirability, and the resultant short-term momentum and long-term mean reversion, the "Wall Street Waltz."

As much as it pains me to admit it, momentum exists. Understanding what it means for rebalancing and asset behavior will make you a better asset allocator.

Summary

1. Money managers do not exhibit consistent stock-picking skill.

2. Nobody can time the market.

3. Because of 1 and 2, it is futile to select money managers on the basis of past performance.

4. Because of 1, 2, and 3, the most rational way to invest in stocks is to use low-cost passively managed vehicles, i.e., index funds.

7

Odds and Ends

No investment guide is complete without a discussion of certain ancillary topics. Now that you've mastered the basics of asset-class behavior and portfolio construction, we'll tie things together with a treatment of the following areas: value investing and the three-factor model, "new era" investing, hedging, dynamic asset allocation, and behavioral finance.

Value Investing

Is it possible to beat the market in the long run? I hope by now that I have convinced you otherwise. A better question can be asked: Are there market segments and subsegments that outperform or underperform relative to their risk? Examples of this have already been presented; the long-term return of precious metals and other "hard assets" (collectibles, precious stones) is trifling compared to their very high risk. More subtly, the risk of owning long-term bonds is much higher than that of short-term bonds, yet their returns are the same. Are there any characteristics of stocks that predict higher or lower expected return? We are already aware of one: company size. As we have seen, small stocks outperform large stocks in the long run. Unfortunately this comes at the cost of higher risk.

Stocks outperform almost all other assets in the long run because you are buying a piece of our almost constantly growing economy. Think of all the technological advances of the twentieth century and the wealth they have created: air transport, radio, television, automobiles, consumer electronics, and computers. You benefit financially from these wonders by owning stock, not T-bills or corporate bonds. So far, so good. Unfortunately, investors then make a fatal extrapolation: that the most profitable stocks to own must be those of the most rapidly growing companies with the hottest products. These are known as "growth companies."

A key investment concept is that of "valuation," i.e., how to tell when an individual stock or stock market is expensive or cheap. (It is a much simpler matter to talk about the valuation of the stock market as a whole or of an individual market sector.)

There are three commonly used measures of individual stock or of aggregate stock market value: price/earnings (P/E) ratio, price/book (P/B) ratio, and dividend yield. Ultimately, you are buying a stock in order to own a piece of its earnings. P/E describes how much you are paying for those earnings. Say XYZ Multimedia, Inc. earns $5 per share and sells for $100 per share. It has a P/E ratio (also called the *multiple*) of 20; you are paying $20 for each $1 of earnings. A company selling at a P/E of 30 is said to be expensive, and one selling at a P/E of 10 is said to be cheap. Unfortunately, company earnings are not particularly stable. Quite frequently the earnings of even the largest and most stable companies disappear entirely, and on rare occasions net corporate profits disappear *for the entire U.S. stock market.* (This happened for a prolonged period during the Great Depression and for a brief period during the early 1980s; the losses sustained by many large U.S. corporations exceeded the profits of the rest, resulting in a net loss for U.S. industry as a whole.) Further, it is easy for corporate accountants to "fiddle" with reported earnings to the point where they are meaningless. For this reason, P/E has only limited value. Ben Graham made the astute observation that corporate earnings provide useful information only when averaged over several years.

All companies have a *book value*; this can be thought of as the net value of a company's total assets, although the accounting reality of this number is much more complex. It is a rough number. The book value of an airline is easily understood; it is primarily the value of its planes, buildings, and office equipment, minus its liabilities. Let's assume ABC Airlines owns assets valued at $2 billion and liabilities of $1 billion, resulting in net assets of $1 billion; let's further assume that the value of all of its outstanding stock is $2 billion. Its P/B ratio is 2; it is selling for twice its book value. A stock with a P/B of less than 1 is said to be cheap; one with a P/B of more than 5 is said to be expensive, at least relative to its book value. The book value of a stock is very stable; corporate accountants usually have no need to fudge this number.

Finally, there is dividend yield. This is easy to understand—it is simply the amount of dividend remitted to the shareholders divided by the price of the stock. If XYZ Multimedia, Inc. sells for $100 per share, earns $5 per share and remits $3 of this to the shareholders, then the dividend yield is 3%. It is possible for a company to pay more in dividends than its earnings, but it obviously cannot do this indefinitely. Small or rapidly growing companies frequently pay no dividends at all; they need to retain all of their profits in order to grow. Until very recently, large, slowly growing companies often paid dividends in excess of 5%.

We are now capable of telling how expensive the tomatoes are. First, it is useful to examine the P/E, P/B, and dividend yield of the entire U.S. stock market. Figure 7-1 plots the P/E of the market over the past 73 years. We see that this number usually varies between about 7 and 20 and averages about 14; in fact, the number can be much larger than this if earnings are near zero because the denominator is so small. When the market P/E is about 7, it is definitely cheap; when it is greater than 20, it is expensive.

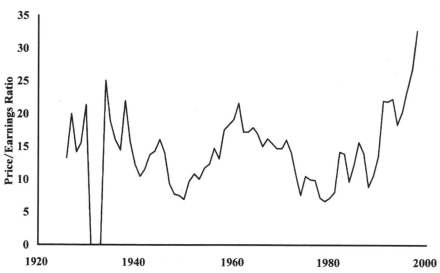

Figure 7-1. Price/earnings ratio, 1926–1998.

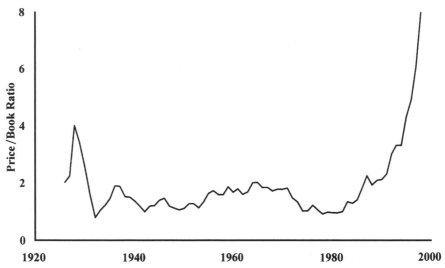

Figure 7-2. Price/book ratio, 1926–1998.

Figure 7-2 plots the P/B of the market. Until recently it had varied between about 1 (cheap) and 3 (expensive); it averages about 1.6. Recently it has ballooned to about 8. Because of the recent data, some have questioned the validity of this measure of expensiveness.

Figure 7-3 plots dividend yield. Historically it has varied between 2.5% (expensive) and 7% (cheap); it averages about 4.5%. The higher the yield, the cheaper the price; the lower the yield, the higher the price. Again, currently stocks yield a historically low 1.3%, and many question its usefulness as well.

Solid data on the ranges of P/E, P/B, and dividend yield are available only for the largest U.S. stocks. For smaller U.S. stocks, the data are more fragmentary, but the ranges of P/E and P/B are similar; dividend yields are considerably smaller. Valuation of foreign stocks is highly problematic because of the differences in accounting standards among nations; nonetheless, the ranges of P/B of most of the EAFE nations seem similar to that of the United States.

We shall see that long-term returns are usually higher when valuations are cheap and lower when they are expensive. Whether this is of any practical use is open to question.

At any one time, some individual stocks are cheaper than others. Is it useful to purchase cheap stocks in preference to expensive ones? There is a very large volume of data that answers this question resoundingly in the affirmative.

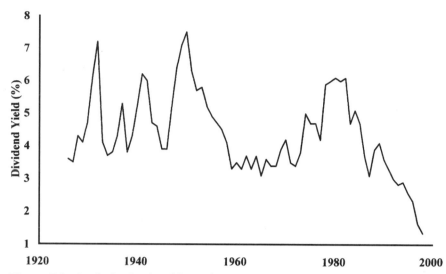

Figure 7-3. Stock dividend yield, 1926–1998.

Studies on Value Investing

The first study of buying cheap stock used a "Dow P/E strategy," similar to the recent, more popular Dow dividend strategy described next. In 1964 Paul Miller, head of research at Drexel & Co., examined buying the 10 lowest P/E stocks of the Dow 30. He published a memorandum in which he summarized the results of this technique for the 28 years from July 1936 to June 1964 (Table 7-1).

Mr. Miller's data was collected in a slightly unusual manner. First, he used July to June fiscal years. Second, the return statistic used was price change only; this does not take reinvested dividends into account. Adding in reinvested dividends would result in actual returns of about 5% higher. These data are clear-cut: The lowest P/E stocks (the ones that everybody hates) greatly outperformed the market, and the highest P/E stocks (the ones that everybody loves) greatly underperformed the market. Does this extra return come at higher risk? This hypothesis is supported by the standard deviation and "worst annual loss" data, which are greater for the low P/E stocks than for the high P/E stocks and the whole Dow Jones 30. The higher SD of the low-P/E stocks is mostly due to the very large gains registered by them in several years. The low-P/E stocks are actually

TABLE 7-1. Value-Stock Performance, 1936–1964

	Dow Jones Industrials, all 30 stocks	Dow Jones Industrials, highest 10 P/E	Dow Jones Industrials, lowest 10 P/E stocks
Annualized price change	+6.54%	+1.50%	+12.18%
Standard deviation	16.3%	15.7%	21.1%
Number of losing years	10	12	7
Number of losses >10%	5	7	2
Worst annual loss	−20.9%	−24.6%	−30.5%

the least risky when looked at from the perspective of the total number of losing years or of losses greater than 10%.

Investors are increasingly seeking higher returns with value stocks, but let's take a step back and see what this means in actual practice. Perhaps the most currently popular method is the so-called Dow dividend strategy, which buys the five highest-yielding Dow stocks. I've listed the five highest-yielding and lowest-yielding stocks at the time of this writing:

Highest yielding	Lowest yielding
Phillip Morris	Wal-Mart
J. P. Morgan	McDonald's
Minnesota Mining	IBM
Chevron	Disney
Eastman Kodak	American Express

Most readers will recognize the high-yielding (cheap) group as "terrible" companies, and the low-yielding (expensive) as "good" companies.

Probably the most impressive work in this area was done by Professors Fama and French, published in the *Journal of Finance* in June 1992. They exhaustively studied stock returns from July 1963 through December 1990 and found that all of the variation in return among stocks could be explained by just two factors: company size (no surprise here) and P/B. They divided their stock database into 10 groups ranging from the lowest P/B (cheapest) to the highest P/B (most expensive). The cheapest one-tenth of the market returned 19.6% annually, and the most expensive tenth, 7.7% annually. The smallest cheapest stocks returned 23% annually. They also found P/E useful, but not nearly as useful as P/B. After taking P/B into consideration, P/E had no predictive value.

Are Ben Graham, Fama, French, and a legion of others all telling us that we shall profit by buying bad companies? Yes. Bad companies are cheap; it is quite possible that management will turn the company around and make them back into "good" companies. Further, even if a bad company's performance worsens, it will not surprise the investment world; the price will probably not drop all that much. On the other hand, good companies are expensive; they are expected to grow to the sky. When, as inevitably happens, they stop growing to the sky, they are taken out and shot by the market. David Dreman has beautifully documented this phenomenon. The largest movements in a company's price usually occur when its earnings either greatly exceed or fall short of analysts' expectations. (Note that in the short term it matters little to the price of a stock whether its earnings are high, low, or negative. What really matters is whether they are higher or lower than the "Street" anticipates; better to have a loss for the quarter which is less than the Street expects than to have great earnings which are less than the Street expects.) Dreman has observed that "value" stocks tend to fall much less in price than "growth" stocks when earnings disappoint. Conversely, "value" stocks tend to rise more in price than "growth" stocks when earnings exceed expectations. To repeat:

Good companies are generally bad stocks, and bad companies are generally good stocks.

This concept is very hard for both small investors and professionals to grasp, and probably underlies the poor performance of most professional money managers. No matter how many finance journals they read, they cannot bring themselves to buy bad companies.

Probably the most vivid example of the good company–bad stock paradigm was provided by the popular 1982 book *In Search of Excellence,* by management guru Tom Peters. He identified numerous "excellent" companies using several objective criteria. Several years later, Michelle Clayman, a finance academic from Oklahoma State University, examined the stock market performance of these companies and compared it with a matched group of "unexcellent" companies using the same criteria. For the five-year period following the book's publication, the unexcellent companies outperformed the excellent companies by an amazing 11% per year. As you might expect, the unexcellent companies were considerably cheaper than the excellent companies by P/E, P/B, and dividend criteria. People naturally assume that good companies are good stocks, when the opposite is true most of the time. Psychologists refer to this sort of syllogistic error as "representativeness."

It has long puzzled academic efficient-market theorists that these popular strategies (low P/E, low P/B, high dividend) have worked so well for so long. They are so well-known that enough people should use them so that their advantage should vanish. The reason why these strategies still work, decades after they were described is simple: Cheap companies are dogs, and most people cannot bring themselves to buy them. Ben Graham wrote *Security Analysis* 50 years ago, which is basically a primer on how to identify cheap, safe stocks. Ben Graham's disciples are among the most successful money managers in the United States. One of them, Warren Buffett, is one of the wealthiest men in the world. By all rights, Graham's method should have long since stopped working, but it continues to work. Everybody wants to own Amazon.com, Microsoft, Intel, and AOL. No one wants to buy Woolworth's.

Value versus Growth

Looking for cheap stocks is called *value investing.* The opposite of this is *growth investing,* looking for companies with rapidly growing earnings. Although there certainly are some very successful growth-stock investors, they have been swimming upstream. You are more likely to swim faster if you head downstream.

Efficient-market theorists are fond of pointing out that there is no pattern to stock or market prices. (As we have already seen, this is not strictly true.) Growth-stock investors believe that they can pick those companies which will have persistent earnings growth and thus reap the benefits of their ever-increasing earnings stream. Unfortunately, established growth companies are very expensive, often selling at P/Es two or three times that of the market as a whole. A company growing 5% faster than the rest of the market and selling at a P/E twice the market's will have to continue growing for another 14 years at that rate before the shareholder is fairly compensated. As we've already seen, stock price movements are essentially an unpredictable "random walk." Interestingly, it turns out that earnings growth also exhibits random-walk behavior; a company with good earnings growth this year is quite likely to have poor earnings growth next year (and vice versa). In other words, this year's growth stock is quite likely to become next year's value stock, at great cost to its shareholders. Contrariwise, a value stock with poor earnings growth will frequently surprise the market with strong earnings growth, with an agreeable change in P/E and price. This typically happens to only a few stocks in a value portfolio in a given year, but the effects on total portfolio performance are still dramatic.

Perhaps the most lucid explanation of the value effect can be found in Robert A. Haugen's *The New Finance: The Case Against Efficient Markets*. Professor Haugen points out that in mid-1993 the 20% of stocks with the highest P/E (growth stocks) had an average P/E of 42.4. This resulted in an earnings yield of 2.36%. (The *earnings yield* is simply the inverse of the P/E—it's the amount of earnings you're buying for each dollar of stock.) The lowest 20% (value stocks) had a P/E of 11.93, or an earnings yield of 8.38%. In other words, when you bought the glamorous growth stocks in mid-1993, you were getting $2.36 in earnings for each $100 invested; when you bought the doggy value stocks, you were getting $8.38. If you are to come out ahead with growth stocks in the long term, their earnings will obviously have to grow over three times larger than the value stocks. Haugen then followed the earnings growth of the growth and value cohorts. While the growth stocks, as expected, experienced higher earnings growth, this advantage decayed over time, and *their dollar earnings never surpassed those of the value group*. In fact, they never even got close; Haugen estimates that each dollar invested in growth stocks leaves you with less than half of the long-term earnings obtainable from value stocks. Again, as Ben Graham said, in the short term the markets are a voting machine, but in the long run they are a weighing machine. And what they are weighing is earnings.

In a paper published in the *Journal of Finance* in December 1994, Josef Lakonishok and colleagues confirmed earlier work demonstrating the superiority of low P/B and low P/E stocks. They also found that sales growth affected future returns; the most rapidly growing companies had the lowest returns. Although Fama and French and Lakonishok and colleagues all agree that low P/B and P/E stocks outperform growth stocks, they disagree as to why. Fama and French are devout "efficient marketeers," and believe that the higher return of value stocks must be due to some sort of associated increased risk. They've had a difficult time explaining to the investment community the precise nature of this risk, but it goes something like this: Value stocks are sick companies. They have weak profitability, earnings growth, and balance sheets. An economic downturn or even a slight breeze may bankrupt them. Because of this increased risk, they must offer higher returns. After all, if both Kmart and Wal-Mart offered the same future return, who would want to own Kmart? Ergo, value stocks are by definition *not* a free lunch.

On the other hand, Lakonishok and colleagues maintain that the higher returns of value stocks come without higher risk, and then present convincing evidence that the risk of value stocks is *lower* than that of growth stocks. In other words, there *is* a free lunch. Wilshire Associates publishes data of the returns of growth and value stock groupings of various company sizes from 1978 (one of the many goodies available in the Morningstar database). For each company size, the value portfolio returns several points more annualized performance than the same company-size growth portfolio, with a considerably *lower* standard deviation. In fact, it appears that value stocks seem to outpace growth stocks precisely because they are less risky. During bull markets growth beats value, but during bear markets value stocks lose much less than growth stocks. At the end of the day, the returns on value stocks may be superior to growth stocks simply because of their more benign bear-market performance.

The Three-Factor Model

The alternative hypothesis, as we've already mentioned, is that there is no excess return without increased risk exposure. This theory is advanced by Fama and French in the form of their *three-factor model*. This simple, yet powerful construct is extraordinarily useful in understanding long-term returns in markets around the globe. Simply put, any stock asset class earns four different returns:

- The risk-free rate, that is, the time value of money. Usually set at the short-term T-bill rate.

- The market-risk premium. That additional return earned by exposing yourself to the stock market.

- The size premium. The additional return earned by owning small-company stocks.

- The value premium. The additional return earned by owning value stocks.

Everyone earns the risk-free rate. So in the Fama-French universe, the only important decision you have to make is how much exposure you want to the other three factors. If you're a complete coward, you have zero exposure to all three and own only T-bills. And if you're a highly risk-tolerant individual, you have maximal exposure to all three and own only small value stocks.

Let's look at each risk factor individually. In Figure 7-4, I've plotted the trailing five-year annualized "market premium" (the return of the CRSP 1-10 Index—roughly the Wilshire 5000—minus the T-bill return) for the past 36 years. Notice that while it has been persistently positive for the past two decades, things were a good deal rockier in the 1960s and 1970s. Over the entire period, the premium was 5.65% annualized. It certainly wasn't a sure thing, being positive in only 78% of the rolling five-year periods.

Is it possible to bear more risk and thus earn still higher premiums? Yes. You can decide to invest in smaller companies, which are more likely to suddenly disappear than large ones. For the past 36 years, the "size premium" (defined as the return of the smallest half of companies on the NYSE minus the largest half) has been 1.71%. I've plotted it in Figure 7-5. Its rolling five-year return has been positive only 53% of the time.

Last, there is the third, and much more controversial, premium, which I've plotted in Figure 7-6. According to Fama and French, if you are a real risk junkie and want to increase your premium payments even further, you can invest in value companies. These are

Figure 7-4. Five-year annualized market premium.

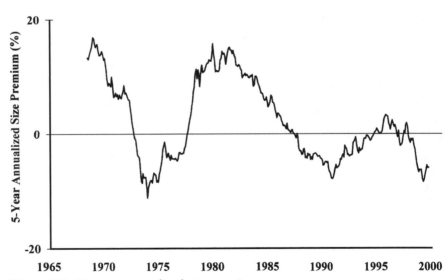

Figure 7-5. Five-year annualized size premium.

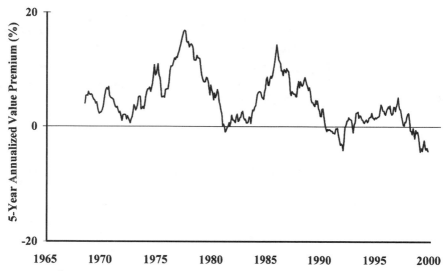

Figure 7-6. Five-year annualized value premium.

the sickest puppies in the litter. Think Harvester, Kmart, Nissan. They are identified by their low valuations, such as price/book ratio. The 36-year premium for investing here (defined as the return of the stocks with the lowest P/B ratios minus the return of the stocks with the highest P/Bs) has been 3.77% annualized. Somewhat surprisingly, as you can see in the plot, this premium has been fairly consistent, being positive 87% of the time. In fact, the reliability of the value premium has caused some to question whether this is not really a free lunch, as opposed to a real "risk story."

These three risk premiums—market, size, and value—have been researched extensively by Fama and French. They, and others, have shown the existence of all three in the U.S. market over a very long time period, as well as in many other countries. Are there other premiums? Probably. There is likely a premium for investing in momentum stocks. The nature of the risk associated with momentum—if any—has yet to be determined.

The three-factor model has another use, which we've previously encountered, and that is the evaluation of money managers. Through the use of sophisticated statistical techniques, it is possible to attribute just how much of a manager's returns can be accounted for by each of the risk factors, and how much, if any, is due to skill. For example, if a manager does particularly well in a given period, it may be because he or she was skillful (or lucky). However, it may also be because the manager was exposed to a market factor that had high returns. As you might already suspect, it turns out that most of the performance of top-ranked managers is due to their factor exposure and that few, if any, of these top-ranked managers actually demonstrate anything which looks like skill in a statistical sense.

Ultimately, the rewards of the capital marketplace go to those who can most intelligently balance the three risk factors, as well as the risks of their employment. A small example: Employees of cyclical, "value" companies should be particularly wary of value portfolios, as in the event of a severe recession both their job prospects and portfolios will suffer disproportionately. Workers who tend to keep their jobs in hard times, like letter carriers and repo men, are in a better position to own value stocks.

Investing in the New Era

The investment climate of the past five years has been so vastly different from that of the prior decades that a discussion of our so-called new era is warranted. As this book is being written, stocks are selling at valuations far higher than ever before seen. Dividend yields of large stocks, which typically range between 3% and 7%, are now 1.3%. P/B ratios, which typically run between 1 and 3, are now 8. And stocks now sell at about 30 times earnings, compared to the historical norm of between 10 and 20. Arguments as to how the old standards don't matter any more, and that we are in a "new era" attempt to rationalize current prices.

So, has the investment paradigm permanently changed? Are the old road markers now useless? Investment paradigms do sometimes shift: In 1958, for the first time in history, stock yields fell below bond yields, and disaster was predicted. None occurred (except for bonds!), and stock yields never again rose above bond yields.

And yet, it is difficult to argue against mathematics and the laws of gravity. In 1958 it could still be pointed out that stock dividends grew over time, whereas bond dividends, being fixed, did not. So it is not unreasonable that bond yields should be higher than stock yields.

But there is no getting around the fact that in the long run equity returns are closely approximated by the sum of the dividend rate, now

1.3%, and the earnings growth rate, historically about 5%. Add these together today and you get an expected stock return of 6.3%. So, in order to justify current valuations one has to postulate that earnings and dividends will begin to rise faster than they have in the past.

No such thing seems to be happening. Go back to Figure 2-11, which plots Dow earnings over the past 80 years. The top surface of the plot is the place to focus. From time to time, recessions and depressions produce sharp downward deviations in earnings, but the upper surface of the plot represents the "full capacity" of corporate earnings. Do you see an accelerating trend the past decade or two? If you do, Mulder and Scully are right outside, and they have some little green men they'd like you to meet.

One often hears the argument that with the accelerating pace of technological change, U.S. companies are on the verge of dramatically increased profitability. A bit of historical perspective is useful. The period from 1830 to 1860 saw the arrival of the two most dramatically transformative inventions in the history of mankind—the steam engine and the telegraph. Within a few short decades, the speed of cross country transportation increased by almost an order of magnitude. Cheap and reliable power became available to manufacturers for the first time in history. Long-distance communication became almost instantaneous. Of course, the past 30 years have also seen wondrous technological innovation. However, consider that today really important news gets from New York to San Francisco only slightly faster than in Grover Cleveland's time and, more likely than not, it takes you and me *longer* to travel cross town or cross country today than it did 30 years ago. Oh yes, the return of U.S. equity from 1830 to 1860 was 4.2%.

In fact, we've heard the new-era argument before—first in 1926–1929, then in the late 1960s. On both occasions, the conventional wisdom was that the old methods of stock valuation had become obsolete and that it was acceptable to pay 50 or 100 times earnings for companies poised on the cutting edge of technological progress. I cannot recommend highly enough Ben Graham's description of the new-era stock market of the 1920s in the recently reprinted 1934 edition of *Security Analysis.* One does not have to change very many words to get a vivid description of today's market frenzy surrounding technology and Internet-related earnings. Just change "100 times earnings" to "100 times sales" and you're there.

Finally, it's worth reflecting on the recent returns of some selected asset classes. For the 10-year period from 1989 to 1998, the return of the Barra Large Cap Growth Index was an astonishing 21.35% annualized; the large-cap value index 16.67%; for 9–10 decile small-cap stocks, 13.2%; and the EAFE index, of foreign stocks 5.54%. The experience of the past decade has convinced many that large-cap stocks have higher returns than small-cap stocks, that growth outperforms value, and that domestic outperforms foreign. As we've seen from more complete historical data, it is likely that none of these assumptions is true.

For those tempted to invest all their money in McDonald's, Coke, Microsoft, and Intel, I've calculated the growth of $1 invested from July 1927 to March 1998 for the most extreme quintiles of small value, small growth, large value, and large growth in Figure 7-7. The annualized returns were 17.47% for small value, 2.18% for small growth, 13.99% for large value, and 10.04% for large growth. One always has to be cautious interpreting historical data. First, they do

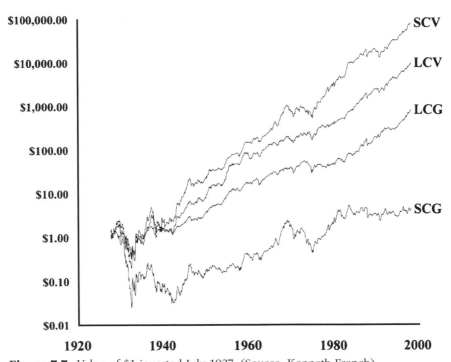

Figure 7-7. Value of $1 invested July 1927. (Source: Kenneth French)

not include the trading expenses detailed earlier in Chapter 6. Second, the pre-1960s data is extremely sketchy in places.

That said, the message is clear: Over the long term value beats growth, and small value may very well beat everything else. The miserable returns for small growth stocks will hopefully come as a wake-up call to those of you considering investing in small technology companies. Recent returns in this area have not been quite that bad, with the real damage being sustained in the pre-1960 era. But clearly, this is an area to be wary of.

In fact, the poor returns of small growth stocks are something of a mystery, as they are even lower than academic theory would predict. My own theory is that there is a "lottery ticket" premium being charged these investors. Just as people purchase lottery tickets, which have a return of about −50%, on the off chance that they may win the grand prize, so too do investors invest in small, rapidly growing companies on the slim chance that they are getting in on the ground floor of the next Microsoft. In other words, this asset class makes up in entertainment value what it lacks in return.

The New Paradigm: Dow 36,000

The new era has recently gotten a persuasive boost from the best-seller list. Writing in the op-ed section of *The Wall Street Journal*, the *Atlantic Monthly*, and more recently their book, *Dow 36,000*, journalist James Glassman and economist Kevin Hassett (hereafter referred to as GH) contend that the market, far from being historically overvalued, is actually ridiculously undervalued. Nervous at Dow 11,000? Get over it. This fearless duo sees fair value at about 36,000.

Their chosen vehicle is the venerable discounted dividend model (DDM), which we have already encountered in Chapter 2. Formulated in 1938 by John Burr Williams, it rests on a deceptively simple premise: Since all companies eventually go bankrupt, the value of a stock, a bond, or an entire market is simply the value of all its future dividends *discounted to the present*. (In GH-speak, this is referred to as the "perfectly reasonable price," or PRP.) Since a dollar of future dividends is worth less than a dollar today, its value must be reduced, or *discounted*, to reflect the fact that you will not receive it immediately. This amount of reduction is called the *discount rate*

(DR). And as we shall soon see, fiddling even a little bit with the DR opens the door to all kinds of mischief.

If this model looks complicated, it is. For each future year you take the present dividend, multiply it by $(1 + g)^n$, where g is the rate of dividend increase and n is the number of years in the future, and then divide by $(1 + DR)^n$. Plus, you have to compute this for an infinite number of years. It can get worse, with two- and three-stage models with varying growth rates over time. But don't sweat the math, because with a constant growth rate the whole infinite sequence simplifies to:

$$PRP = (div)/(DR - g)$$

where PRP = perfectly reasonable price
        div = annual dividend amount
        DR = discount rate
        g = dividend growth rate

If the Dow throws off about $150 per year in dividends, and if you optimistically assume (as GH do) that dividends are growing at 6% per year, then the only other number left to toss into the above equation is that pesky DR. And amazingly, throughout much of the book GH maintain that the appropriate DR is the Treasury bond rate, which at the time was 5.5%. Because the growth rate is greater than the DR, an infinite value for the market results (because in this case the discounted dividend rises each and every year, *ad infinitum*), which even they find hard to swallow. (What the authors missed is that their 6% dividend growth rate covered a period when inflation was around 4%–5%, while the recent 5.5% rate for Treasury bonds presumably reflects a considerably lower future inflation rate.) So lower the dividend growth to 5.1%, keep the DR at 5.5%, and abracadabra, the above equation yields Dow 37,500:

$$PRP = 150/(.055 - .051) = 150/.004 = 37,500$$

Per finance convention, the numbers in the denominator are expressed as decimals, where .055 refers to the DR of 5.5%, and .051 to the dividend growth rate of 5.1%. Notice how tiny the denominator of .004 is relative to the input numbers. Move both of the numbers in the denominator the wrong way by just 1% (.01) and you have a Dow PRP of 6250. And if that displeases you, make your estimates

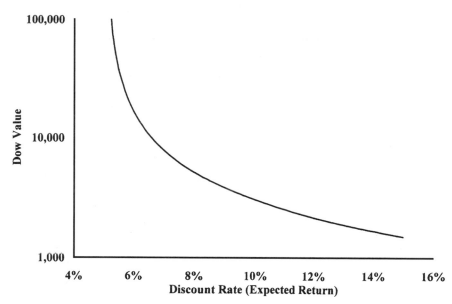

Figure 7-8. 1999 dividends = $150, growth = 5.1%.

just a hair more optimistic, and you get a Dow PRP of infinity. In other words, using the GH model, you can make the PRP of the Dow whatever you want it to be by moving the discount rate and growth rate a smidgen in either direction.

The Glassman-Hassett model is akin to balancing an elephant on a fence post: One small wobble in the post and several thousand pounds will lurch in an unexpected direction. This is evidenced by Figure 7-8, which shows the Dow's value using the Glassman-Hassett growth assumptions over a range of discount rates.

To reiterate, the value of the DR is critical. For example, if the actual DR is 8% instead of 5.5%, then fair value for the Dow falls to 5172. Oops. The same thing happens if the dividend growth estimate is off. As already mentioned, the 6% dividend growth of the past two decades included over 4% of inflation. In other words, real growth was less than 2%. So the dividend growth rate going forward may be quite a bit lower than it has been in the past. Decreasing dividend growth by 2.5% has the same effect as increasing the DR by the same amount—Dow 5172.

So what determines the appropriate DR? It is very simply two things: the cost of money (or the risk-free rate) plus an additional amount to compensate for risk.

Think of the DR as the interest rate a reasonable lender would charge a given loan applicant. The world's safest borrower is the U.S. Treasury. If Uncle Sam comes my way and wants a long-term loan, I'll charge him just 6%. At that DR the DDM predicts that a perpetual $1 annual loan repayment, or coupon, is worth a $16.67 loan.

Next through the door is General Motors. Still pretty safe, but not as riskless as Uncle Sam. I'll charge them 7.5%. At that DR a perpetual $1 repayment/coupon is worth a $13.33 loan.

Finally, in struts Trump Casinos. Phew! For the risk of lending these clowns my money I'll have to charge 12.5%, which means that The Donald's perpetual $1 repayment/coupon is worth only an $8 loan.

So the DR we apply to the market's dividend stream hinges on just how risky we think the market is. And here things get really sticky. Relying on long-term data, GH observe that the stock market is actually less risky than the long Treasury bond. For example, since 1926 the worst 30-year annualized return for common stocks was 8.47% versus only 1.53% for Treasuries.

Of course, a very different picture emerges when one looks at shorter periods. For example, the worst one-year returns are −43.35% for stocks and −7.78% for bonds. And at a gut level, no matter how much of a long-term investor you think you are, the market still probably got your attention on October 19, 1987.

So the GH-Dow controversy depends on whether you think that investors experience risk as a short-term or a long-term phenomenon. What the authors are saying is that U.S. investors have abruptly lengthened their risk time horizon:

> Seventy years ago few investors understood that excessive trading undermines profits, that stock-price fluctuations tend to cancel themselves out over time, making stocks less risky than they might appear at first glance, and that it is extremely difficult to outperform the market averages. Americans have learned to buy and hold.

One wonders what planet GH inhabit. Are they unaware that trading volume has been steadily increasing for decades, not decreasing? That average domestic mutual fund turnover has increased from 30% to over 90% in the past 25 years? That a recent survey of over 66,000 accounts at a large West Coast discount brokerage showed an average annual portfolio turnover of 75%? That only 7% of mutual fund investments are indexed? That the historically modest market declines of 1987, 1990, and 1997, far from resulting in inflows from legions of long-termers buying cheap, produced dramatic mutual fund outflows? Most authoritatively of all, in an elegant study published in the *Quarterly Journal of Economics* in 1995 Shlomo Benartzi and Richard Thaler calculated that the risk horizon of the average investor was just *one year.*

The easiest way of thinking about the interplay of short- and long-term risk is to imagine a new kind of 30-year Treasury bond, similar to the conventional bond, *except that the government stands ready at all times to redeem it at par* (face value). Clearly, the redeemable bond would carry a considerably higher price and lower yield because it is immunized against the shock of a short-term increase in rates. And yet on the GH planet, where investors only care about long-term return, it would be priced identically to the conventional 30-year bond, since both have the same return to maturity.

Even conceding GH's point that investors are increasingly focused on stocks for the long run and will manage to push the Dow up past 36,000, one has to ask just how free of risk stocks would be at that point. The authors ignore a rather inconvenient fact: that recent market history has dramatic effects on DR. In 1928, just as today, everybody was a "long-term investor," and the DR for stocks was quite low (although probably not as low as it is today). Five years later, with the attrition rate of buy-and-holders approaching 100%, the DR was dramatically higher. And at Dow 36,000, it wouldn't take much of a change in the DR in order for the risk-free world of stocks to come to an abrupt end. If investors decided that they demanded even a measly 1% risk premium, the Dow would decline by about two-thirds. The irony being that to the extent GH are right about a near-term "correction" of stock prices past 36,000, the risks of subsequent stock ownership increase dramatically.

Ignoring the crash scenario still does not make the GH planet look very appetizing. For the DR has another, even more profound significance. Namely, that *the DR of an asset is the same as its expected return.* If the true discount rate is 5.5% and the Dow is correctly priced at 36,000, then the future return of stocks is also 5.5%. Assuming inflation averages 2.5% over the next 30 years, that's a real return of just 3%. Why would any rational investor invest in stocks priced to a 3% real return with Treasury Inflation Protected Securities (TIPS) priced to produce a guaranteed 4% real return?

There are other, more fundamental problems with Dow 36,000. For starters, consider the significance of a 5.5% long-term stock return. The "cost of capital" for corporations is necessarily the same as this long-term return. At a dirt-cheap capital cost of 5.5%, corporations are not going to be particularly careful about how they spend it. The free-spending behavior of the dot-coms, whose capital comes even cheaper, is not encouraging. (Or, on a grander scale, just how careful is Uncle Sam with his 5.5% capital?)

That said, on rare occasions investment paradigms do dramatically and permanently shift. We've already mentioned what happened in 1958, when for the first time stock yields fell below bond yields. At the time there was an almost universal outcry from financial pundits that this was an unnatural state of affairs and that stock prices were destined to fall, once again raising their yields, so as to restore the old order. And yet the stock market never looked back; prices continued to rise, and stock yields fell even farther below bond yields. (New paradigms can also be painful. The year 1958 also brought the start of a bear market in bonds much worse than anything seen since the time of Alexander Hamilton.) Today, stocks yield a full 4%–5% less than bonds. So I would not dismiss *Dow 36,000* out of hand. But some skepticism is in order. (Even the authors themselves admit that they could be wrong, and thus hold about 20% of their assets in bonds.)

Hedging: Currency Effects on Foreign Holdings

The holder of a foreign stock or bond is subject not only to the intrinsic risks of that security but also to the additional risk of currency fluctuation. For example, a bond denominated in U.K. pounds will rise or fall in value along with the value of that currency relative to the dollar. This currency risk can be eliminated (*hedged*) by selling forward a pound contract in the futures market at nominal cost. In the real world, you must first buy something before you sell it. But in finance, you can often sell something first before buying it back later; this is called *selling forward* (and is similar to "shorting" a stock).

A currency contract that is sold forward increases in value as that currency falls, and vice versa. The resultant hedged bond generally has considerably lower risk than the unhedged bond, since the currency value change in the bond is exactly counterbalanced by the opposite change in value of the futures contract.

However, the situation with foreign *stocks* is much more complicated. Consider the 20 years ending October 1999. The annualized standard deviation for hedged European stocks (Morgan Stanley Capital Index-Europe) was 14.92% for the period. (The hedged index is the return that a European investor would see in the native currency. It is also called the *local return*.) The past decades have been an extremely turbulent time in the foreign exchange markets, with the monthly returns of the European currencies themselves experiencing an annualized SD of 10.44%. However, because this currency return is uncorrelated with the stock return, the SD of the dollar-denominated European market was just 16.25%— only slightly higher than that of the hedged (local currency) index. It is in fact not difficult to find short periods where hedging actually *increased* the risk of a European stock portfolio.

By now, of course, you are sophisticated enough to know that just because unhedged foreign stocks are slightly more risky than the hedged variety, this does not imply adverse portfolio behavior. In order to examine this problem, I looked at the behavior of three assets for the November 1979 to October 1999 period: the broad U.S. market (represented by the CRSP 1-10 Index) and the hedged and unhedged MSCI-Europe. One problem becomes immediately apparent—the returns for the three assets are somewhat different. The hedged European index yielded a 13.43% return, with the currency return boosting the unhedged portfolio's return to 15.18%. And, as we saw in Chapter 4, during the 1980s and 1990s the domestic U.S. return was much higher—in this case 17.21%. During this period, then, hedging and foreign exposure were both highly detrimental, and the best portfolio was almost exclusively domestic.

To correct these biases I adjusted the unhedged European and domestic portfolio returns down to the 13.43% level of the hedged European portfolio, and looked at the return-versus-risk characteristics of the various U.S. and European mixes in Figure 7-9. As can be seen, the hedged portfolios (the loop on the left) have both lower return and lower risk than the unhedged portfolios (the loop on the

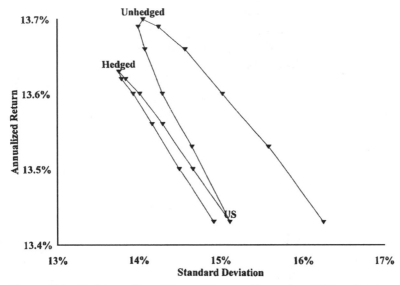

Figure 7-9. Hedging effect, U.S. and Europe, November 1979 to October 1999.

right). In any case, note the very narrow vertical returns scale—we are talking about less than a dozen basis points difference. So all things being equal, hedging European stocks is a wash. But, of course, in the real world things are never equal. It is quite likely that currency exposure may turn out to be either highly beneficial or detrimental in the coming years. And we can't predict which in advance.

Fortunately, the advantages of hedging (lower individual asset risk, positive hedging return) and disadvantages (higher correlation with the rest of the portfolio) largely offset each other; in the very long run there is not that much difference in risk and return characteristics of hedged-versus-unhedged portfolios. Over shorter periods, however, the differences can be considerable. For example, during the rapid depreciation of the dollar that occurred in 1984–1986 and 1994–1995, unhedged portfolios greatly outperformed hedged portfolios. The opposite occurred when the currency cycle unwound in 1998–1999.

For those few people who are planning to spend their retirement in Europe or Japan, their eventual risk may be lessened by not hedging. In other words, since their liabilities will be in foreign currency, the chance of having sufficient funds to meet their needs is increased by not hedging.

Math Details: The Hedging Hall of Mirrors

To complicate things even more, the cost of hedging needs to be considered as well. At the institutional level of mutual funds, the fees, commissions, and opportunity costs associated with hedging are minimal, perhaps no more than a few dozen basis points. The real cost of hedging has to do with the nature of forward currency contracts. As this is being written, the spot and six-month forward contracts for the pound, yen, and deutsche mark are as follows:

	Pound	Yen	Deutchemark
Spot rate	$1.6239	$0.009758	$0.5219
Six-month forward rate	$1.6245	$0.010052	$0.5288
Forward premium	0.04%	3.01%	1.32%

When you purchase a hedge, you "sell short" the forward rate and buy it back at a later date. If you sell short the six-month forward contract and wait until just before it expires six months later to buy it back, you will be buying the currency (or "covering the short position") at the spot rate. If the spot and forward rates do not change in the interim, you will earn a profit equal to the *forward premium*, which is the difference between the spot and forward rates. This is negligible in the case of the pound, 3.01% for the yen, and 1.32% for the deutsche mark. In effect, you are being paid to hedge these currencies. (This is because at the present time interest rates are lower in each of these countries by an amount equal to the forward premium rate. If you wished to hedge an unstable currency with high interest rates, such as the ruble, the forward premium would be highly negative, with a very high hedging expense.)

And, if you own stocks or bonds exactly equal to your hedging amount, you will earn the forward premium no matter what happens to the exchange rate, as long as the forward premium stays intact.

(Continued)

Math Details (Continued)

You would think that the forward rate would be predictive of the future exchange rate. It isn't. For example, the reason that the yen forward premium is so high (3% over six months, or 6% per year) is that Japanese interest rates are so low. What the forward premium seems to be saying to the U.S. holder of a Japanese five-year bond (currently yielding only 1%) is: "Don't worry about the low yield, you'll make up the difference with a 6% annual currency appreciation." In fact, however, exchange rate history suggests that on average this doesn't happen. Over the past several decades, global bond managers have made excess returns purchasing unhedged high-yielding bonds of developed nations with negative forward spreads, reaping advantage when the underlying currency fails to depreciate as much as forecast by the forward spread. This market inefficiency is probably the result of the fact that governments are major players in the currency game; governments are different from individual and institutional investors in that their primary goal is not profit, but rather currency defense.

Lastly, hedging cost needs to be considered when evaluating historical data. As pointed out by Jeremy Siegel in *Stocks for the Long Run*, in 1910 the pound was worth $4.80. It has since fallen to one-third that value. One might think that hedging the currency would have increased one's return from British stocks. Wrong. Since for almost all of that period British interest rates were higher than those in the United States, the hedging costs were considerable; you'd have been much better off not hedging.

The question of how much currency hedging is best is one of the thorniest questions faced by investors; neither mean-variance analysis nor spreadsheet analysis provides any clear-cut answers. As a practical matter this decision has already been made for you. All of the foreign stock index funds recommended in Chapter 8 are unhedged, and the only low-cost foreign bond funds are hedged. And, as we've already seen, this is not a bad state of affairs.

More importantly, be aware that the degree of hedging strongly affects the short-term performance of foreign stock and bond mutual funds; do not be too upset if one or more of your funds has a bad year simply because they were completely hedged with a falling dollar, or vice versa. As long as your funds stick to their hedging policies, you will be rewarded when the currency pendulum swings the other way, which it almost always does.

Dynamic Asset Allocation

Dynamic asset allocation refers to the possibility of varying your policy allocation because of changing market conditions. After spending much of this book convincing you of the virtue of fixed allocations, why am I relaxing this valuable discipline so late in the game? Isn't changing the policy allocation tantamount to market timing, a demonstrably profitless activity?

Before proceeding further, let me be clear: Adherence to a fixed policy allocation with its required periodic rebalancing is hard enough. It takes years to become comfortable with this strategy; many lose their nerve and never see the thing through. You cannot pilot a modern jet fighter before mastering the trainer; likewise, you should not attempt dynamic asset allocation before mastering fixed asset allocation.

In the 1995 version of this book, I provided an example of how changing the stock and bond allocation in the opposite direction of P/B produced a slight improvement in risk-adjusted return. Alas, this is no longer true, as a P/B sensitive investor would have completely exited the stock market by last year. However, for what it's worth, Figure 7-10 is a graph of P/B versus five-year forward average return. Although there is some scatter, there is obviously a strong tendency for returns to be high with low starting P/Bs, and low with high P/Bs. The most remarkable aspect of this plot is that the lower boundary of the data points forms quite a straight line; this represents the minimum return which can be expected for a given P/B. At a P/B of 1.5, an average five-year return of about 2% seems guaranteed; at a P/B of 1.25, 7.5%, and at 1.0, a return of 13% seems assured. Is this a useful relationship? That's anybody's guess. However, Figure 7-10 is a good reminder that when stocks get more expensive, their future

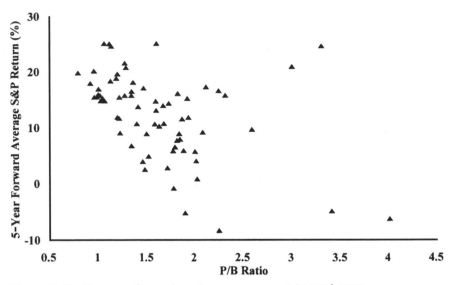

Figure 7-10. Five-year forward stock returns versus P/B 1926–1993.

returns are likely to decline, and that when stocks are very cheap, future returns are likely to be more generous.

However, it is still not a bad idea to occasionally change your allocation slightly in the opposite direction from valuation. If two years ago you thought that a 6% exposure to emerging markets was appropriate, perhaps with the recent carnage in this area 7% or 8% might not be inappropriate. If three years ago you were holding 40% S&P 500, perhaps 35% might not be a bad idea in the current bubbly environment. Think of it this way—when you rebalance your portfolio in order to maintain your target allocation, you purchase more of an asset that has declined in price, and thus gotten cheaper. When you actually increase the target portfolio weighting of an asset when its price declines and it gets cheaper, you are simply rebalancing in a more vigorous form—you are "overbalancing." A simpler way of overbalancing is to increase your target allocation ever so slightly—perhaps by 0.1% for every percent that the asset falls in value, and vice versa.

Dynamic asset allocation gets a bad rap because most investors change their allocations around in response to changes in economic or political conditions. As we have discussed, this is a poor approach. In the author's opinion, changes in allocation that are purely market-valuation driven are quite likely to increase return. Rebalancing requires nerve and discipline; overbalancing requires even more of both of these scarce commodities. Very few investors, small or institutional, can carry it off.

Behavioral Finance

The overarching premise of this book is that rational investors, faced with the facts of modern investing, will make certain logical decisions and choices. There's only one problem. Human beings are not rational. The past few decades have seen an explosion in the field of *behavioral finance*—the study of the logical inconsistencies and foibles that plague investors. Three human behavioral phenomena are worth discussing: *overconfidence, recency* (which we have already mentioned), and *risk aversion myopia.*

Overconfidence

For those of you with a congenital dislike of public radio, for nearly two decades show host, writer, and (dare I say it) singer Garrison Keillor has produced *A Prairie Home Companion,* set in the mythical town of Lake Wobegon, Minnesota. (A small confession: I listened to the show for over two years before nagging doubts sent me to my Rand McNally.) Mr. Keillor is heard to intone at the beginning and end of each show that in Lake Wobegon, "all the women are strong, all the men are good-looking, and all the children are above average."

Well, on Wall Street everyone's above average too. In a piece on investor preconceptions in the September 14, 1998, "Abreast of the Market" series in *The Wall Street Journal,* writer Greg Ip examined the revision in investor attitudes with the market decline in the summer of 1998. He tabulated the change in investors' return expectations as follows:

Expected returns	June 1998	Sept. 1998
Next 12 months, own portfolio	15.20%	12.90%
Next 12 months, market overall	13.40%	10.50%

The first thing that leaps out of this table is that the average investor thinks that he or she will best the market by about two percent. While it is possible that many investors may in fact beat the market by a few percent, it is of course mathematically impossible for the average investor to do so. In fact, as we've already discussed, the average investor must of necessity obtain the market return, minus expenses and transaction costs. Even the most casual observer of human nature should not be surprised by this paradox—folks tend to be overconfident

Overconfidence likely has some survival advantage in a state of nature, but not in the world of finance. Consider the following:

- In one study, 82% of U.S. drivers considered themselves in the top 30% of their group in terms of safety. (In Sweden, not unsurprisingly, the percentage is much lower.)

- In another study 81% of new business owners thought they had a good chance of succeeding, but that only 39% of their peers did.

- Several housewives from Beardstown form an investment club, incorrectly calculate their portfolio returns, and then write a best-seller describing the reasons for their "success."

The factors associated with overconfidence are intriguing. The more complex the task, the more inappropriately overconfident we are. *Calibration* (receipt of results) of one's efforts is also a factor. The longer the feedback loop between our actions and their calibration, the greater our overconfidence. For example, meteorologists, bridge players, and emergency room physicians are generally quite well calibrated. Most investors are not.

Recency

The second surprising piece of data from the above table of return expectations was that in September 1998, after prices had fallen by a considerable amount, investors' estimates of stock returns were *lower* than they were in June. This is highly irrational. Consider the following question: On January 1, you buy a gold coin for $300. In the ensuing month the price of gold falls, and your friend then buys an identical coin for $250. Ten years later, you both sell your coins at the same time. Who has earned the higher return?

Very few investors would not chose the correct answer—your friend, having bought his coin for $50 less, will make $50 more (or at worst, lose $50 less) than you. Viewed in this context, it is astonishing that any rational investor would impute lower expected returns from falling stock prices. The reason for this is what behavioral scientists call *recency*—we tend to overweight more recent data and underweight older data, even if it is more comprehensive. Had any conversations lately with someone with less than five years' investing experience and tried to convince him that he cannot expect 20% equity returns over the long term? Blame recency. Make the recent data spectacular and/or unpleasant, and it will completely blot out the more important, if abstract, longer-term data.

All very interesting, you say, but of what use are such metaphysics? First and foremost, it explains why most investors are "convex" traders. This is a term coined by academicians William Sharpe and Andre Perold to describe "portfolio insurance" strategies in which equities are bought as prices rise and sold as they fall. A "concave" strategy represents the opposite—buying as prices fall and selling as they rise. Although some may find one or the other strategy more appealing, Sharpe and Perold make a more profound point: In a world populated by concave traders, it is advantageous to be a convex trader, and vice versa. Financial history in fact suggests that because of recency the overwhelming majority of equity investors are convex—when prices rise, investors' estimates of returns irrationally rise, and they buy more. If indeed most investors exhibit such convex behavior, then the rational investor is concave. (Bond investors, on the other hand, appear to be less subject to recency, and thus a bit less convex, probably because falling bond prices make the most overt feature of a bond, its current yield, more immediately attractive to the investing public.)

Risk Aversion Myopia

Human beings experience risk in the short-term. This is as it should be, of course. In the state of nature, our ancestors' ability to focus on the risks of the moment had much greater survival value than a long-term strategic analytic ability. Unfortunately, a visceral obsession with the here and now is of rather less value in modern society, particularly in the world of investing.

Overemphasis on the possibility of short-term loss is referred to as *risk aversion myopia*. In Chapter 2, after looking at the long-term superiority of stocks over bonds, you might have found yourself asking the question, "Why doesn't everybody buy stocks?" Clearly, in the long term, bonds are actually *more* risky than stocks; there is no period of more than 30 years in which stocks did not outperform bonds. In fact, many academicians refer to this as "the equity risk-premium puzzle"—why stocks have been allowed to remain so cheap that their returns so greatly and consistently exceed that of other assets. The answer is that our primordial instincts, a useless relic of millions of years of evolutionary history, cause us to feel more pain when we suddenly lose 30% of our liquid net worth than the more damaging possibility of failing to meet our long-term financial goals. How bad is the problem? I've already mentioned the immensely clever article by Shlomo Benzarti and Richard Thaler (one of behavioral finance's brightest stars) which examined the interaction of the risk premium and investor preference. They estimated that the risk horizon of the average investor, was about one year. Myopic indeed.

Socrates told us that the unexamined life is not worth living. For the modern investor, failure of self-examination can be as damaging to the pocketbook as to the soul.

Summary

1. Bad companies are usually good stocks, good companies are usually bad stocks. Value investing probably has the highest long-term returns.

2. Currency hedging has important effects on short-term portfolio behavior, but little in the way of long-term impact.

3. It is permissible to change your allocation slightly from time to time, as long as you do so in a direction opposite from valuation changes.

8

Implementing Your Asset Allocation Strategy

There is a memorable passage from the movie *Full Metal Jacket*, about the experiences of a Marine unit in Viet Nam. The story centers on a callow young journalist who falls in with a group of grizzled veterans. The Marine Corps has a dialect all its own; after a few minutes of banter a top sergeant turns to the journalist and challenges him with, "I see you can talk the talk, but can you walk the walk?" Understanding the theory of asset allocation is easy; pulling it off is another matter.

Choosing Your Allocation

By now you should have a fairly good idea of what your basic allocation should look like. If you don't, I shall walk you through the process. This is essentially a recapitulation of the Chapter 5 discussion, except that I've changed the order of the steps:

1. *Determine your basic allocation between stocks and bonds.* First, answer the question, "What is the biggest annual portfolio loss I am willing to tolerate in order to get the highest returns?" Table 8-1 summarizes the process of determining your risk tolerance.

   In previous versions of the book, I allowed the most risk-tolerant investors 100% equity exposure. At the present time, however, it appears that expected stock and bond returns going forward may not be all that different, and a dollop of bonds is recommended for all investors.

   The percentage stock recommendations in Table 8-1 will need to be revised downward depending on your time horizon. Your

Table 8-1. Allocating Stocks versus Bonds

I can tolerate losing _____% of my portfolio in the course of earning higher returns:	Recommended percent of portfolio invested in stocks:
35%	80%
30%	70%
25%	60%
20%	50%
15%	40%
10%	30%
5%	20%
0%	10%

maximum stock allocation should be 10 times the number of years until you will have to spend the money. For example, if you need the money in two years, your stock allocation should not exceed 20%; if you will need the money in seven years, it should not exceed 70%.

2. *Determine how much complexity you can tolerate.* Is keeping track of six different asset classes more than you can handle? Or are you an "asset-class junkie" who craves a portfolio of exotic birds such as Pacific Rim small companies or emerging markets value exposure?

For starters, you'll need at least four asset classes:

- U.S. large stocks (S&P 500)
- U.S. small stocks (CRSP 9-10, Russell 2000, or Barra 600)
- Foreign stocks (EAFE)
- U.S. short-term bonds

If this is all you can handle, fine. The above four classes will provide you with most of the diversification you'll need. However, if you can tolerate the added complexity, I'd recommend breaking things down a bit further:

- U.S. large stocks—market and value
- U.S. small stocks—market, value, and REITs
- Foreign stocks—Europe, Japan, Pacific Rim, emerging markets, and small cap
- U.S. short-term bonds

3. *Determine how much tracking error you can tolerate.*   Are you the kind of investor who mentally compares his returns on a frequent basis with that of the Dow or S&P 500? Do you get depressed when your stock allocation doesn't do as well? Then perhaps you should consider an allocation heavy in large-cap U.S. stocks, whose performance will not vary greatly from that of the domestic benchmarks.

Planning for Taxes

Somewhere in the last few paragraphs, without realizing it, we ran into an enormous obstacle called "taxes." If all of your assets are in tax-sheltered vehicles such as an IRA, Keogh, 401(k), 403(b), private pension plan, or annuity, then this is not a problem. But if a significant part of your assets is taxable, extreme care is called for. For example, the S&P 500 is a relatively tax-efficient index, but the small-cap indexes are another story. These benchmarks, and the funds that track them, have relatively high turnover. Worse, stocks usually move out of a small-cap index, and thus need to be sold, after a large price appreciation places them into the mid- or large-cap category, generating disproportionately large amounts of capital gains. The same is true of foreign small-cap stocks.

This also occurs with value index funds—both large and small cap. The major reason for a stock's moving out of the value category is that a price rise often places the stock in the growth category. Again, unwanted capital gains distributions are the result.

REITs present an even worse problem. Because most of their return is the result of dividends, they are taxable at your full marginal rate, and thus are very likely not appropriate for taxable accounts.

Finally, bonds present similar tax problems. Depending on your state of residence, a municipal bond fund or Treasury ladder may be advantageous.

Indexing: Vanguard and DFA

At this point, we are finally able to consider individual investment vehicles. In the previous versions of the book, I took a more eclectic attitude toward individual fund selection, but recent events have made things a good deal simpler because a wide variety of indexed investment products have become available from the leaders in the field: Vanguard and Dimensional Fund Advisors (DFA).

The structure of the Vanguard Group is unique in the mutual fund industry; it is owned entirely by its individual funds, and thus by its shareholders. In other words, the profits of the entire mutual fund group are distributed back to the funds themselves, and thus to you, the investor. Almost all other mutual fund providers are owned by their company stockholders, or else are privately owned: profits from the funds' management most defintely do *not* flow to the funds' shareholders. This is a critical distinction; most mutual fund companies are rewarded by charging (some would say milking) their fund's shareholders high management fees. The concept of the "expense ratio" is central to mutual fund investing. A fund's expenses incurred by accounting, shareholder servicing, and investment management fees are subtracted from the return that the fund actually earned on its investments. The average expense ratio of a U.S. stock fund is 1.32%, and for foreign funds it is near 2%. Moreover, as we saw in Chapter 6, the expense ratio is just the beginning, with commissions, spreads, and impact costs further lowering your returns. Of course, Vanguard also incurs these costs, but because of low index fund turnover, these expenses are much less than that of conventional actively managed funds.

Here are the Vanguard stock funds I'd recommend:

1. *Vanguard 500 Index Fund.* The granddaddy of all index funds, which tracks the S&P 500. Sometime in the next year, it will almost certainly become the planet's largest mutual fund. A fine choice for the long haul, particularly in tax-sheltered accounts, it does have some modest drawbacks for the taxable investor. Standard & Poor's periodically adds and deletes stocks from the index, incurring distributions as the fund rearranges its portfolio accordingly. Because of this, I'd recommend two alternatives for the taxable investor—the Vanguard Total Stock Market Index Fund and the Vanguard Tax-Managed Growth and Income Funds.

2. *Vanguard Tax-Managed Growth and Income Fund.* This tax-managed version of the 500 Index Fund seeks to minimize distributions by selling high-basis-cost shares first and selling other positions at a loss to offset gain sales. Note should be made of the

fund's higher minimum ($10,000 versus the usual $3000) as well as a 2% redemption fee for shares held less than one year and a 1% fee for shares held less than five years.

3. *Vanguard Total Stock Market Index Fund.* This fund tracks the Wilshire 5000 Index (which now includes more that 7000 stocks) and is particularly suitable for taxable investors. As it owns "the whole market," it sells a stock only if the company is bought out for cash. It can be thought of as constituting 75% large cap, 15% mid cap, and 10% small cap.

4. *Vanguard Value Index Fund.* This fund tracks the bottom 50% of market capitalization of the S&P 500 when sorted by price/book ratio. This peculiar division of the S&P 500 results in about 380 value stocks and 120 growth stocks, because the latter have much higher market capitalizations than the former. Because this strategy results in high turnover, it is not suitable for taxable accounts. I suspect that Vanguard will be coming out with a tax-managed large-cap value strategy sooner or later, but they're not there yet.

5. *Vanguard Small-Cap Index Fund.* This fund tracks the Russell 2000 Index. It is suitable only for tax-sheltered accounts.

6. *Vanguard Tax-Managed Small-Cap Fund.* For taxable accounts, this fund uses the tax-managed strategy described above. This fund has a $10,000 minimum and the same 1% or 2% redemption fee as the Tax-Managed Growth and Income Fund. It also carries a .5% purchase fee, payable to the fund itself to mitigate the spread and impact costs in this area.

7. *Vanguard Small-Cap Value Index Fund.* This fund is suitable for tax-sheltered accounts only because it is likely to have high turnover and distributions. It has a .5% purchase fee. Vanguard does not yet have a tax-managed small-cap value fund.

8. *Vanguard European and Pacific Stock Index Funds.* These funds have a low turnover and are suitable for taxable accounts. The Pacific Stock Index Fund is essentially a Japanese fund, with Japan comprising almost 80% of fund assets.

9. *Vanguard Emerging Markets Stock Index Fund.* Because of the very high spreads and transactional costs, there is a .5% purchase fee and a .5% redemption fee. It is uncertain how much in distrib-

utions the fund will yield in the long term, and thus how suitable it will be for taxable accounts. However, Vanguard has a history of keeping fund transactions at a minimum, and it is sensitive to the high trading costs in this area.

10. *Vanguard Total International Stock Index Fund.* This is the one for those of you who prize portfolio simplicity. It is suitable for taxable accounts. There is also a Tax-Managed International Fund with the same $10,000 minimum and redemption fee schedule as the other tax-managed funds, plus a .25% purchase fee.

11. *Vanguard REIT Index Fund.* Because almost all of the long-term return of REITs comes from dividends, this asset class should be used only in the tax-sheltered setting. There is a 1% redemption fee for shares held less than one year.

Although it's tough to beat Vanguard for indexed asset-class coverage, there are a few holes, particularly in the tax-managed value department. In addition, Vanguard lacks international small-cap and international value vehicles. If you must have exposure to these areas, then you will need Dimensional Fund Advisors. Based in Santa Monica, DFA's strategies are designed by some of the brightest stars in academic financial economics, including Gene Fama, Ken French, and Rex Sinquefield. DFA offers almost any index fund you can think of: U.S. large stocks; U.S. large-value stocks; international large stocks; international large-value stocks; U.S. small stocks; U.S. small value-stocks; international small-value stocks; U.K., Japanese, Continental, and Pacific Rim small stocks; as well as emerging markets small-cap and value stocks. In addition, DFA offers foreign and domestic tax-managed value funds. DFA's expenses are almost as low as Vanguard's. DFA funds are available through an approved financial advisor, who will of course charge you a fee. Further, you will have to buy its funds through one of the "supermarkets" (Schwab, Vanguard, or Waterhouse), where transactions will run $24–$50 a pop. Still, if you must have these asset classes, you may find it worthwhile to canvas financial advisors for one who will charge a reasonable fee for the service.

Small-cap international exposure is a particular problem. In previous versions of this book, I recommended Acorn International and Tweedy Browne Global Value funds for this purpose, and in fact these choices have done quite well over the past few years. The only problem is that they're really not small-cap funds. In spite of their relatively small median-market-caps ($1035M and $2543M per Morningstar, April 1999), they correlate much more highly with the various (large-cap) Morgan Stanley Capital Indexes, and even the S&P 500, than a small foreign fund should. Thus, the real reason why those two funds have performed so well is that they are, in fact, medium to large—and not small—foreign funds. If you want authentic exposure to international small caps, you have the choice of dealing with DFA through a financial advisor or waiting for Vanguard to come out with an international small-cap fund.

Table 8-2 summarizes the Vanguard and DFA index funds appropriate for both taxable and tax-sheltered investing, for tax-sheltered only investing, and taxable only (tax-managed) investing. Some of you will notice the absence of growth index funds in the above list. In spite of the recent superb results of large-cap growth investing, I believe that, in the long run, growth investing is a bad idea, particularly in the small-cap arena. In any case, the S&P 500 and small-cap indexes, being capitalization weighted, are for all practical purposes growth proxies.

A new development in the world of indexing are so-called exchange-traded funds (ETFs). These come in many sizes and shapes. The most popular are spiders (SPDRS), based on the S&P 500. Unlike mutual funds, these securities trade like stocks on the American Stock Exchange. They have both advantages and disadvantages relative to a conventional index fund. On the plus side, they can be traded throughout the day, as opposed to a conventional fund, which is priced only at the end of the trading day. SPDRS do not generate appreciable capital gains and are thus slightly more tax-efficient than conventional S&P index funds as well. On the other hand, the purchase and sale of an ETF incurs both commissions and spreads, and so is slightly more expensive to own. Also, ETFs reinvest dividends only quarterly, and thus will suffer a slight performance drag relative to a conventional fund, which continuously reinvests its dividends. On the whole, unless you are an active trader, ETFs hold no real advantage over a conventional index fund. There is also an exchange-traded fund, QQQ, aimed at the Nasdaq 100 index, and several new SPDRS that track S&P sector indexes. Also

Table 8-2. Stock Index Fund Summary

Tax-sheltered and taxable	Tax-sheltered only	Taxable only (tax-managed)
Vanguard	*Vanguard*	*Vanguard*
500 Index	Value Index	Tax-Managed Growth and Income
Total Stock Market Index	Extended Market Index	Tax-Managed Small-Cap
European Stock Index	Small-Cap Index	Tax-Managed International
Pacific Stock Index	Small-Cap Value Index	
Emerging Markets Stock Index	REIT Index	
	Total International Stock Index	
DFA	*DFA*	*DFA*
U.S. Large Company	U.S. Large-Cap Value	Tax-Managed U.S. Marketwide Value
Large-Cap International	U.S. 6-10 Small Company	Tax-Managed U.S. 5-10 (small) Value
	U.S. 6-10 Small Company	Tax-Managed US 6-10 Small Company
	U.S. 9-10 (micro) Small Company	Tax-Managed International Value
	Real estate	
	International Value	
	International Small Company	
	International Small-Cap Value	
	Small Company	
	Pacific Rim Small Company	
	U.K. Small Company	
	Continental Small Company	
	Japanese Small Company	
	Emerging Markets	
	Emerging Markets Small-Cap	
	Emerging Markets Value	

available are ETFs that index various foreign markets, known as World Equity Benchmark Securities, or WEBS. Here a much clearer recommendation can be made—stay away. Over the past several years, WEBS have underperformed their national market indexes by an average of 2% per year because of excessive expenses and turnover. Although WEBS offer certain theoretical advantages over the Vanguard and DFA foreign index funds relating to portfolio rebalancing, in practice these potential advantages are outweighed by their expense disadvantage.

The coming years will see an explosion in the asset-class varieties offered by ETFs that may in the long run prove a boon to the passive asset-class-based investor. However, before purchasing one of these vehicles I'd make sure that it has not trailed its benchmark index by more than its expenses for a period of at least one or two years and that its expenses are not excessive.

Bonds

Here things separate out much more cleanly into taxable and nontaxable bonds. As this is being written, consider the yields on the following Vanguard short-term (2-3 year maturity) bond funds: Short-Term Corporate Fund, 5.95%; Short-Term Treasury Fund, 5.25%; and Limited-Term Tax-Exempt Fund, 3.71%.

For the tax-sheltered investor, this is a no-brainer—you go with the highest-yielding Short-Term Corporate Fund. For the taxable investor, things are a bit more complex. Assume that you are in the 36% marginal federal bracket and your state imposes a 5% income tax. The Treasury Fund is subject to the federal but not the state tax, and yields 3.36% after tax. The Tax-Exempt Fund is subject to the state but not the federal tax, and yields 3.52% after tax. The Corporate Fund is subject to both, and yields 3.62% after tax. Thus, at the present time, short-term corporate bonds have a slight advantage. However, this relationship changes from month to month and over varying maturities.

At the present time the situation with respect to foreign bond funds is highly unsatisfactory. For starters, because of Chairman Emeritus Bogle's dislike of currency exposure, Vanguard offers no low expense international bond funds. Probably the best is Standish, International Fixed-Income Fund, but this has a minimum of $100,000, or $10,000 when bought through certain supermarkets. It is fully hedged and has a reasonable expense ratio of 0.53%. American Century and T. Rowe Price offer largely unhedged funds with lower minimums but higher expenses (about 0.8%). Dimensional Fund Advisors has two fine short-term global bond funds (hedged) with reasonable expenses, if you decide to go that way. Presently, European and Japanese government bond yields are actually lower than available from the U.S. Treasury, and it hardly seems wise to pay 12%–20% of the average coupon in expenses for these funds.

My overall advice with respect to federal, corporate, and municipal bond funds is to use Vanguard's short-term and intermediate-term offerings. Consider a Treasury ladder, which I'll shortly discuss, if you have at least $50,000 to commit to this area. Stay away from foreign bond funds unless you are already a DFA client or until such time as Vanguard enters this area.

Treasury Ladders

Finally, those of you with more than $50,000 in bond assets should consider a Treasury ladder. Treasury bonds can be bought at auction with no spread through most brokerage houses. Consider that a $25 commission on the purchase of a five-year note for $20,000 amounts to just 0.125% of the purchase price, or to a total expense of 0.025% per year for your own personal Treasury "mutual fund." Purchasing five-year (and initially some two-year and one-year) notes at regular intervals will result in a steady stream of maturing securities. Further, it is possible to purchase Treasuries at auction without any commission under certain circumstances. Fidelity Brokerage, for example, does not charge a commission for auction purchases over $20,000, and Vanguard does not charge an auction-purchase commission for their "Flagship" accounts ($750,000 total family assets). Finally, it is also possible to buy Treasuries at auction directly from Uncle Sam (Treasury Direct), but the bonds bought in this manner are not easily available for sale before maturity, if necessary.

Treasuries are considered to be riskless, and the gap between Treasury and corporate yields can be considered the "price of safety." When this gap is small, safety is cheap, and Treasuries should be purchased.

Determining Your Precise Allocation

In Chapter 5, we studied several different portfolios arranged according to risk, complexity, and conventionality. By now you should have some idea of where you fit along these three dimensions of portfolio construction. However, we did not consider the value dimension, nor did we consider the effects of taxation.

Of critical importance to your allocation is the relative amount of tax-sheltered versus taxable assets. On the one extreme, if all of your assets are in an IRA or pension plan, the tax consequences of your investment strategy matters not at all. You may use whatever asset classes you like, and rebalance however often you like.

On the other hand, if all of your assets are taxable, you are operating under extreme asset-class constraints, but this also makes things very simple. You are limited to the asset classes in the first and last columns of Table 8-2, which include just eight Vanguard index funds. Basically you are back to U.S. large, U.S. small, and foreign.

The most complex situations are where you have substantial amounts of both tax-sheltered and taxable assets. The strategy here is to put the most tax-efficient asset classes (the first and last columns of Table 8-2) in your taxable accounts and the least tax-efficient asset classes (middle column, basically small and large value, and REITs) in your tax-sheltered accounts.

To give you an idea of how this is done, let's consider the case of an investor with $200,000—$100,000 each in taxable and tax-sheltered (IRA) accounts. Using the above principles, policy the investor has decided on the following policy allocation:

15% U.S. large market

10% U.S. large value

5% U.S. small market

10% U.S. small value

5% European

5% Pacific

5% Emerging markets

5% REITs

20% Municipal bonds

20% Short term corporate bonds

Using Table 8-2 for the stock funds, he decides to use the following Vanguard funds and place them in the appropriate taxable or tax-sheltered account:

Taxable Account

15% Total Stock Market Index Fund

5% Tax-Managed Small-Cap Index Fund

5% European Stock Index Fund

5% Pacific Stock Index Fund

20% Limited-Term Tax-Exempt Fund

IRA Account

10% Value Index Fund

10% Small-Cap Value Index Fund

5% Emerging Markets Stock Index Fund

5% REIT Index Fund

20% Short-Term Corporate Fund

Notice how the investor has segregated the most tax-efficient assets into the taxable account, and the least tax-efficient assets into the IRA.

Executing the Plan

From a purely financial point of view, it is usually better to put your money to work right away. However, if you are not used to owning risky assets, then getting started is a little like taking your first swim in the lake on Memorial Day. It is not a good idea to jump right in—better to wade in very slowly in order to get used to the icy water. From a practical point of view, it takes quite a while to accommodate yourself to the ups and downs of the market. It also takes some time to convince yourself that rebalancing is a good idea, particularly as you find yourself pouring cash into a prolonged bear market for one, several, or all of your assets.

The traditional way of reaching a fully invested position is by *dollar cost averaging (DCA)*. It involves investing the same amount regularly in a given fund or stock, illustrated as follows. Assume that a mutual fund fluctuates in value between $5 and $15 over a given period, and that $100 is invested three times at prices of $10, $5, and $15. Now, the average price of the fund over the purchase period is $10, but using DCA, a lower average price is actually obtained. Here's how: We purchased 10 shares at $10, 20 shares at $5, and 6.67 shares at $15, for a total of 36.67 shares. The average price was thus $8.18 per share ($300/36.67), because we purchased more shares at the lower price than at the higher price.

DCA is a wonderful technique, but it is not a free lunch. Buying those 20 shares at $5 took great fortitude, because you were buying at the "point of maximum pessimism." Security prices do not get to bargain levels without a great deal of negative sentiment and publicity. Think of what it felt like to be buying stocks in October 1987, junk bonds in January 1991, or emerging markets stocks in October 1998, and you'll know what I mean. Do not underestimate the discipline that is sometimes necessary to carry out a successful DCA program. On the other hand, the real risk of DCA is that your entire buy in period may occur during a powerful bull market, which may be immediately followed by a prolonged drop in prices. Such are the uncertainties of equity investing. Always remember that you are compensated for bearing risk, and buying during a prolonged bull market is certainly a risk.

There is an even better method of gradually investing, known as *value averaging*, (VA), described by Michael Edleson. Professor Edleson produced two editions of a book by that title, and unfortunately they are both out of print. A simplified version of his technique is as follows. Instead of blindly adding, say, $100 per month, one draws a "value-averaging path," consisting of a target amount, which increases by $100 per month. In other words, one aims at having $100 in the account in January, $200 in February, and so forth, out to $1,200 by December of the first year, and $2,400 by December of the second year. In this case, we are not simply investing $100 per month; this will happen only if the fund does not change value. If the fund value declines, then *more* than $100 will be required; if the fund goes up, then less will be required. It is even possible that if the fund value goes up a great deal, no money at all will have to be added in some months.

Further, assume that we plan an investment of $3,600 over three years. Using VA, we will probably not complete our $3,600 investment in exactly 36 months. If in general the markets are up, it may require another three or six or nine months to complete the program. If, on the other hand, there is a bear market, then we will run out of money long before 36 months is up.

Let's now return to our investor with $200,000 to invest in the above assets. Right off the bat, he has a problem. His allocation to the Vanguard Tax-Managed Small-Cap Fund is 5%, or $10,000, which is the minimum investment amount for this fund. Further, the minimum initial investment for the other Vanguard funds is a $3000 in taxable accounts and $1000 in IRAs. Table 8-3 displays a value averaging path for the above strategy.

At the beginning of the period, the amounts not invested in the initial fund minimums are placed in the Limited-Term Tax-Exempt Fund and Short-Term Corporate Fund for the taxable and IRA accounts, respectively, from which further contributions to the stock funds are drawn.

This method, in my opinion, is about the best technique available for establishing a balanced allocation, but it is not perfect. As already pointed out, if there is a global bear market, you will run out of bond reserves long before 36 months are up. The opposite will happen if stock prices rise dramatically. It is also possible, in fact, quite likely, that after a time the taxable and tax-sheltered halves of our allocation will get out of kilter. What happens, for example, if there is a dramatic bull market in emerging markets stocks, while at the same time European and Pacific stocks fall significantly? In that case, there is no problem with selling some of the tax-sheltered Emerging Markets Stock Index Fund and purchasing additional European and Pacific shares. This means that we will wind up with more than our 20% allotment of bonds in the IRA and less than 20% in the Limited-Term Tax-Exempt Fund, but this is a relatively minor imperfection.

However, if the opposite happens, we have a more serious problem. If the Pacific and European shares rise significantly, what do we do? If we are still in the VA phase, and building up a position in these assets, then we will simply have to wait a few months before the "value path" eventually rises above our asset level, requiring further purchases. What if this happens after we have completed our VA program? In that case, selling shares of these funds to get back to "policy" would have serious tax consequences and should probably be avoided. About the best we can do is to avoid reinvesting distributions as a slow "safety valve" for these overpriced assets.

Value averaging has many strengths as an investment strategy. First and foremost, the investor is investing at both market lows and market highs; one buys many more shares at the low point than at the high point, which produces significantly higher returns. Second, it gives the investor the experience of investing regularly during times of market pessimism and fear—a very useful skill indeed. VA is very similar to DCA, with one important difference: It mandates investing larger amounts of money at market bottoms than at market tops, increasing returns even further. You can think of it as a combination of DCA and rebalancing. (Value averaging works just as well in reverse; if you are retired and in the distribution phase of your financial life cycle, you will be selling more of your assets at market tops than at bottoms, stretching your assets further.)

Of course, there is no reason why you have to use DCA or VA. Let's assume that you have had a high stock exposure for years and are well-acclimated to financial risk and loss. There is no reason not to plunge right in and fully reallocate your assets according to your new plan.

Please note that there is also nothing sacred about monthly funding over three years—this is merely an example. You can use quarterly, weekly, or even daily funding if you are a whiz with spreadsheets. I'd recommend a minimum of two to three years for funding, however; if market history is any guide, you should have an authentic bear market (or at least correction) during this time. This will enable you to test your resolve with the relatively small mandated infusions and to ultimately convince yourself of the value of rebalancing.

Once you have transferred all of your cash and bonds into your desired allocation, it becomes a simple matter to periodically rebalance the account back to the policy, or "target," compositions. How often should you do this? Again, that depends on whether your assets are in a tax-sheltered or a taxable account.

Rebalancing in a Tax-Sheltered Account

How often do you rebalance your portfolio? If you are investing in a tax-sheltered account, you can do so as often as you wish, since there are no tax consequences. In this instance, what is the optimal

Table 8-3. Sample Value Averaging Path

	Taxable				IRA			
Month	Total SM	TMSC	European	Pacific	Value	SCV	Emg. Mkt.	REIT
1	$3,000	$10,000	$3,000	$3,000	$1,000	$1,000	$1,000	$1,000
2	$3,771	$10,000	$3,200	$3,200	$1,543	$1,543	$1,257	$1,257
3	$4,543	$10,000	$3,400	$3,400	$2,086	$2,086	$1,514	$1,514
4	$5,314	$10,000	$3,600	$3,600	$2,629	$2,629	$1,771	$1,771
5	$6,086	$10,000	$3,800	$3,800	$3,171	$3,171	$2,029	$2,029
6	$6,857	$10,000	$4,000	$4,000	$3,714	$3,714	$2,286	$2,286
7	$7,629	$10,000	$4,200	$4,200	$4,257	$4,257	$2,543	$2,543
8	$8,400	$10,000	$4,400	$4,400	$4,800	$4,800	$2,800	$2,800
9	$9,171	$10,000	$4,600	$4,600	$5,343	$5,343	$3,057	$3,057
10	$9,943	$10,000	$4,800	$4,800	$5,886	$5,886	$3,314	$3,314
11	$10,714	$10,000	$5,000	$5,000	$6,429	$6,429	$3,571	$3,571
12	$11,486	$10,000	$5,200	$5,200	$6,971	$6,971	$3,829	$3,829
13	$12,257	$10,000	$5,400	$5,400	$7,514	$7,514	$4,086	$4,086
14	$13,029	$10,000	$5,600	$5,600	$8,057	$8,057	$4,343	$4,343
15	$13,800	$10,000	$5,800	$5,800	$8,600	$8,600	$4,600	$4,600
16	$14,571	$10,000	$6,000	$6,000	$9,143	$9,143	$4,857	$4,857
17	$15,343	$10,000	$6,200	$6,200	$9,686	$9,686	$5,114	$5,114
18	$16,114	$10,000	$6,400	$6,400	$10,229	$10,229	$5,371	$5,371
19	$16,886	$10,000	$6,600	$6,600	$10,771	$10,771	$5,629	$5,629
20	$17,657	$10,000	$6,800	$6,800	$11,314	$11,314	$5,886	$5,886
21	$18,429	$10,000	$7,000	$7,000	$11,857	$11,857	$6,143	$6,143
22	$19,200	$10,000	$7,200	$7,200	$12,400	$12,400	$6,400	$6,400
23	$19,971	$10,000	$7,400	$7,400	$12,943	$12,943	$6,657	$6,657

24	$20,743	$10,000	$7,600	$7,600	$13,486	$13,486	$6,914	$6,914
25	$21,514	$10,000	$7,800	$7,800	$14,029	$14,029	$7,171	$7,171
26	$22,286	$10,000	$8,000	$8,000	$14,571	$14,571	$7,429	$7,429
27	$23,057	$10,000	$8,200	$8,200	$15,114	$15,114	$7,686	$7,686
28	$23,829	$10,000	$8,400	$8,400	$15,657	$15,657	$7,943	$7,943
29	$24,600	$10,000	$8,600	$8,600	$16,200	$16,200	$8,200	$8,200
30	$25,371	$10,000	$8,800	$8,800	$16,743	$16,743	$8,457	$8,457
31	$26,143	$10,000	$9,000	$9,000	$17,286	$17,286	$8,714	$8,714
32	$26,914	$10,000	$9,200	$9,200	$17,829	$17,829	$8,971	$8,971
33	$27,686	$10,000	$9,400	$9,400	$18,371	$18,371	$9,229	$9,229
34	$28,457	$10,000	$9,600	$9,600	$18,914	$18,914	$9,486	$9,486
35	$29,229	$10,000	$9,800	$9,800	$19,457	$19,457	$9,743	$9,743
36	$30,000	$10,000	$10,000	$10,000	$20,000	$20,000	$10,000	$10,000

Total SM = Vanguard Total Stock Market Index Fund

TMSC = Vanguard Tax-Managed Small-Cap Fund

rebalancing frequency? Recall that the major effect of rebalancing on return is the *rebalancing bonus*, the excess return obtained from buying low and selling high that rebalancing forces. Rebalancing can be regarded as the only consistently effective method of market timing. What we are really asking is: What rebalancing period produces the greatest rebalancing bonus? The answer is complex but basically hinges around finding the interval for which the aggregate correlation among portfolio assets is lowest and annualized variances the highest. In other words, the asset variances and correlation coefficients during a given period are different depending upon what return intervals are being used: e.g., daily, weekly, monthly, quarterly, annually. The interval with the lowest correlations and/or the highest variances is the optimal rebalancing period. I've seen optimal rebalancing periods ranging from monthly to as long as once every several years for similar portfolios. There is probably no way to predict in advance which rebalancing period will be optimal for a given portfolio, but as a general rule, long rebalancing intervals are preferred. This is because of the momentum phenomenon discussed in Chapter 7; asset-class returns have a slight tendency to trend, and it is best to take advantage of this characteristic. In other words, above- or below-average asset-class performance has a tendency to persist, and it is best to let such behavior run its course for a while before rebalancing. If you're having trouble with the rebalancing concept, don't feel bad. It's a very complicated area and is often misunderstood by even the most sophisticated players. The easiest way to think about the rebalancing interval problem is to imagine a portfolio consisting only of U.S. and Japanese stocks. Since the former has headed nearly straight up and the latter nearly straight down over the past decade, rebalancing as rarely as possible (perhaps every 10 years!) would have been preferable to doing so frequently. If you rebalance every year or two, you probably won't go too far wrong.

Rebalancing Your Taxable Accounts

More definite recommendations can be made regarding rebalancing taxable accounts: Do so as sparingly as possible. In fact, a good case can be made for *never* rebalancing, considering the capital gains jolt you will get each time you do. First and foremost, selling your taxable stock and bond funds triggers capital gains taxes at the federal and state level. Second, frequently buying and selling taxable mutual funds can be an accounting nightmare, although Vanguard and a few other fund companies have made life quite a bit easier with year-end share-tracking reports. Even the most tax-efficient index funds have *some* year-end distributions. If a particular taxable fund exceeds its policy target, at least avoid reinvesting these distributions. Instead, take the distribution in cash, so it can be rebalanced elsewhere. It is fine to add frequently to a taxable mutual fund, but I'd recommend selling at most once per year. Remember to meticulously file and save your transaction slips and account statements. The opinion of your accountant should definitely be sought in these matters.

Does It Have to Be This Complex?

This book is aimed at the investor who wishes to squeeze every bit of return possible out of a given degree of risk. As we have seen, the essence of this involves splitting your portfolio into many small imperfectly correlated parts. This may seem distastefully complex to some readers. The traditional all-U.S. half-stock and half-bond portfolio is extremely simple and easy to rebalance. Vanguard even offers single funds which will provide various mixes of U.S. stock and bond indexes. For this convenience, you are probably sacrificing 1% to 2% of long-term return for a given degree of risk.

Another compromise would be to split your stock component equally into six Vanguard index funds (Value, 500 Index, Small-Cap, European, Pacific, and Emerging Markets) for your stock component and use one of their short-term bond funds for the fixed-income component. Even simpler, Vanguard offers a Total International Index Fund. For those who value the convenience of simple portfolios, these compromises may be worthwhile. (One caveat about the Vanguard Total International Fund: It is a "fund of funds" and thus not eligible for the foreign tax credit. I recommend the new Vanguard Tax-Managed International Fund for this purpose.)

The Everything Fund

Is it possible to find a single fund which will relieve you of all of the trouble of asset allocation? Sure—the mutual fund industry is nothing if not responsive to every whim of the investing public. There are many funds which will provide you with what they consider to be the "optimal" asset allocation; these are called, naturally, *asset-allocation funds*. There are a few problems with these funds. First, they have not been around for very long, so it is hard to evaluate them. Second, what little track record they do have is not particularly impressive. The average 10-year annualized return (for April 1988–March 1999) of Morningstar's asset-allocation and global funds was 10.79%, compared with 17.70% for the broadly based Wilshire 5000, and 9.08% for the Lehman Long Bond Index. Even more amazingly, it was almost precisely the same as the 10.80% returned by the MSCI World Index, in spite of the fact that this benchmark started out the period with about 40% Japanese equity, which subsequently returned −4.11% annually. In other words, the average asset-allocation fund will do about as well as the worst possible indexed global allocation.

It would be nice if Vanguard offered a reasonable global index fund, but they do not. Their asset-allocation funds (Wellesley, Wellington, Asset Allocation, Life Strategies, STAR, and Global Asset Allocation) have the disadvantage of being grossly underweighted in foreign and small stocks. I do not recommend any of these funds. Lastly, Vanguard may get its act together and come out with an "everything index fund" comprising all of the world's investable assets, now that Mr. Bogle, who dislikes foreign assets, has retired. Stay tuned.

For those wishing to use one or two funds, I make the following recommendation with some trepidation. The Tweedy, Browne firm has a long record of consistent value investing; one could easily split one's investments between their American and Global Value funds. They have a distinguished record in private money management, but have been in the mutual fund business for less than six years. They have done very well, but their expenses are fairly high; I'd keep an eye on them. I would also use them only in tax-sheltered accounts. The dangers of recommending actively managed funds are vividly illustrated by the "one-stop" choices provided in a previous version of this book: SoGen International and Mutual Discovery. The former has fallen flat on its face, and the latter has lost its star manager (Mike

Price) and has been gobbled up by that faceless conglomerate known as Franklin Resources. I'd like to believe that the same will not happen to Tweedy, Browne, but if history is any guide, it probably will.

Keeping Abreast of Market Valuation

In Chapter 7 we discussed dynamic asset allocation—changing your policy allocation from time to time in line with asset valuations. Don't try this one at home, unless you have rebalanced successfully through at least a few market cycles. If you do get to that point, remember, increase your allocation of an asset only after it has gotten measurably cheaper and only after it has been hammered in price. Never increase your allocation to an asset because of economic or political events or because you have heard an analyst make a convincing case for doing so. The same goes for decreasing your allocation in a given area: Do so only because its valuations have gotten much higher after a major run-up.

Even if you have no intention of ever changing your policy allocations, it is still a good idea to become informed about market valuations. By far the easiest way to do this by purchasing Morningstar's Principia mutual fund database. Then, look up the P/E, P/C (price/cash flow), P/B, and dividend yield for the relevant index funds:

Vanguard 500 Index (S&P 500)

Vanguard Value Index

Vanguard Growth Index

Vanguard Small-Cap Growth Index

Vanguard Small-Cap Value Index

Vanguard Small-Cap Index (Russell 2000)

Vanguard Extended Market Index (Wilshire 4500)

Vanguard Total Market Index (Wilshire 5000)

Vanguard European Stock Index (EAFE-Europe)

Vanguard Pacific Stock Index (EAFE-Pacific)

Vanguard Emerging Markets Stock Index (MSCI-EM index)

DFA U.S. 9-10 Small Company (very small U.S. stocks)

DFA U.K. Small Company

DFA Emerging Markets

DFA Japanese Small Company

DFA Continental Small Company

DFA Pacific Rim Small Company. (Southeast Asia, Australia, and New Zealand)

If you're not willing to pay for Principia, then Barra's Web site provides a multitude of valuation parameters for a broad range of domestic (but not foreign) assets. As discussed above, P/B and dividend yield are the most stable measurements, with P/E and P/C being of less use. Dividend yield is the only measure that has any meaning across different stock asset classes.

It is always a good idea to know how expensive the tomatoes are; keeping abreast of the above measures is the best way to do this. Each time I get a new Morningstar disk, the first thing I do is print out the valuation parameters for all of the above funds and file it away. By following P/B and dividend yield over time, it is easy to see just how cheap or expensive an asset class has become.

How expensive are the tomatoes right now? As expensive as they have ever been. The P/B of the S&P is currently 10.5. It has never been even remotely this high except once before—in 1929. The dividend yield is also at a record low 1.3%. The historical data on U.S. small stocks and foreign large stocks do not go back very far, but the P/B of these areas (about 3 for small cap, and 4 for foreign) is also probably very high by historical standards. By P/B criteria, small foreign stocks seem cheaper (at 2.4); whether this is a useful piece of information is anybody's guess, as there is not much information about the historical range of P/B for this asset class. Many now assert that P/B and dividend yield have become irrelevant. However, at market highs, one always hears arguments about how the old valuation measures don't matter any more. In fact, it is impossible for market valuations to go to very high levels without a widespread belief that the old yardsticks are broken. Maybe they are, but it is worth remembering the legendary John Templeton's admonition that the four most expensive words in the English language are "this time it's different." (The author will add the five dumbest words: "The bull market remains intact.")

Retirement—The Biggest Risk of All

This book is focused primarily on the investment process, particularly the establishment and maintenance of efficient allocations. Asset allocation in retirement is no different, except that you will primarily be using your withdrawals to control your allocations, as opposed to deposits and rebalancing.

However, there is a risk peculiar to retirement called "duration risk." In order to explore this, let's start with the simplest and least risky of all investments, a one-year Treasury bill. A bill is in reality a zero-coupon bond, bought at a discount. For example, a 5% bill will sell at auction for $0.9524 and be redeemed at par ($1). If a few seconds after it is issued yields suddenly rise to 10%, the bill falls in price to $0.9091, with an immediate loss of 4.55% in value.

But if our investor holds the bill to maturity, he or she will receive the full 5% return, the same as if there had been no yield rise and price fall. And beyond one year, it's all gravy—our investor can now reinvest the entire proceeds at double the yield. The "point of indifference" is thus the one-year maturity of the bill; before one year the investor is worse off because of the yield rise and price fall; after one year, the investor is better off.

Now consider a holder of a 30-year 5% Treasury *bond*. If soon after purchase at par we see the same rise in yield to 10%, our hapless investor has received a financial kick in the solar plexus—the bond is now worth less than 53 cents on the dollar. (The reason is that almost the entire value of the bond is represented by the subsequent 5% coupon payments, worth only half of the current 10% market yield. This is precisely what happened to bondholders between 1967 and 1979.) However, a bond is a very different beast than a T-bill: It throws off coupons that can be reinvested at the higher yield. Because of this, the recovery from disaster takes considerably less than 30 years. In fact, it only takes our hapless bondholder 10.96 years to break even. This 10.96-year period is known in financial circles as the *duration* of the security, and for a coupon-bearing bond it is always less than the *maturity*, sometimes considerably so. (For a zero-coupon bond, maturity and duration are the same.)

There are lots of other definitions of duration, some dizzyingly complex, but "point of indifference" is the simplest and most intuitive. (The other useful definition is the ratio of price-to-yield change. That is, our 30-year bond will decrease 10.96% in price with each 1% increase in yield.) Duration is also an excellent measure of the risk of an investment. The higher the duration, the bigger the risk. To reiterate, *after 10.96 years, our unlucky bondholder is better off for the fall in price because of the rise in yield*.

Duration is almost always used to describe bonds, but there is no reason why you can't apply the same concept to stocks as well. It's a simple matter to model the duration of the stock market. For example, stocks are currently yielding about 1.3%. If they decline 75%, the absolute amount of the dividend remains the same, but you are now investing those dividends at a yield that is four times higher—5.2%. Eventually this will redound to your benefit, and you will wind up better off than at the lower yield and higher price. How long does it take to catch up? It depends on the beginning yield and the magnitude of the decline. With today's 1.3% stock yield, a 25% decline would have a duration of 63 years; a 50% decline, 51 years; a 75% decline, 33 years; and a 90% decline, only 19 years.

Skeptics will point out that a 90% stock decline would likely be associated with a decrease in the absolute dividend amount, but even during the Great Depression the real dividend stream of the Dow decreased by only 25%. In fact, the 1929–1933 bear market provides a superb reality check of the above paradigm. One dollar invested in stocks on Labor Day 1929 declined in value to 16.6 cents by Independence Day 1932 and increased back to par by the end of January 1945—less than 13 years after the bottom.

The dividend yield was 2.6% in September 1929, and for the 30 years after that, earnings growth was only 1.8%. Thus, had the crash not occurred, only then would stocks have returned 4.4% per year, resulting in a break-even point with what actually occurred in January 1952, or 22 years later, almost exactly the same period predicted by the duration model. Viewed from this perspective, today's market is a good deal more frightening than that of 1929, since a 75% stock decline produces a duration of 19 years at the 2.6% 1929 yield, versus 33 years at the current 1.3% yield.

Certainly, such a wrenching market decline today would wreak havoc on the financial and social structure of the republic, as it did 70 years ago. But at the same time, today's high prices and resultant low yields are no great blessing either. This is because the lower the coupon or dividend yield, the longer the duration. Thus, the lower the yield, the higher the market price; the longer the duration, the greater the risk.

Is there a way that individuals can shorten the duration of their stock portfolio? Yes. Since the size of the yield influences duration (the greater the yield, the shorter the duration), you can effectively increase the yield of a portfolio by adding to it every month. Let's begin with the 1.3% yield, 75% price fall, and 33-year-duration scenario referred to above. If you start with $10,000 and neither add nor withdraw from your account, you will break even at the 33-year duration. But continuously add in $200 per month and you break even at just over 11 years.

The expedient of shortening your stock and bond duration with additional investment is of course not available to you in retirement; retirees can be devastated if the duration of their stock and bond holdings is longer than their retirement horizon.

For the truly long-term investor, the results of a prolonged bear or bull market may very well prove of little consequence or may even produce surprisingly paradoxical results. But in reality, equanimity to market declines depends on time horizon. If you're retired and living off savings, you will neither have enough time to get over the duration hump nor be able to make the contributions to shorten it. If you're a boomer who is still adding to a decent-sized nest egg, then you will likely have plenty of time. And if you're a twenty-something just beginning to save, then get down on your knees and pray for a market crash.

There can be no question that investors experience risk as a short-term phenomenon. When we think about investment pain, the first thing that comes to mind is a brutal bear markets which leaves our portfolio considerably lighter than they were a few months or years before. But, as we've seen, time heals almost all asset-class wounds, and the biggest risk that we face is simply that we will run out of money before we shuffle off our mortal coil. After all, most of us are saving and investing for a purpose, usually retirement, or some other well-defined future financial need. The ivory-tower types refer to this as *shortfall risk*, and it's worth a few pages of consideration. (We've already talked in Chapter 7 about how investors tend to obsess on short-term risks and rewards, while ignoring the more important longer-term picture.)

There are easily available retirement calculators which can help you determine this risk, but it's important for you to develop an intuitive feel for the problem. Let's start with an estimate of your before-tax needs. Assume that you've determined that you need, in addition to your Social Security, $40,000 in annual income. It's best to simplify the calculation by factoring out inflation by using *real*, or inflation-adjusted, investment returns. That way you are always dealing with current, constant purchasing-power dollars. As we've already discussed, a reasonable estimate for the real return of a mixed stock and bond portfolio is somewhere in the neighborhood of 4%. That means that you should be able to spend 4% of your portfolio each year while maintaining its real value indefinitely. And if you can maintain the portfolio's real value indefinitely, so too can you maintain the real value of your withdrawals. In that case, you will need $1,000,000 in assets, since 4% of $1,000,000 is $40,000. In other words:

Required savings = income requirement/real investment return

= $40,000/0.04 = $1,000,000

This calculation assumes that you wish to keep your principal intact. If you are willing to expire on schedule after 30 years with zero assets, you will need less. Using the annuity/mortgage function on a financial calculator, such as a Texas Instruments BA-35 (about $20 at most discount stores), we come up with required savings of only $691,681.

These calculations vividly demonstrate the extreme importance of keeping investment expense under control. The 4% return assumption refers to the *market return*, from which investment fees and other expenses have to be subtracted. If your retirement account or 401(k) plan uses the typical assortment of fund choices bearing 1%–2% total expenses, then you may need up to twice as much ($40,000/0.02 = $2,000,000) in retirement savings than if you had used low-cost index funds. This kind of calculation emphasizes the extreme importance of attention to expense—in this situation, 2% of additional costs translates into a doubling of your retirement savings requirement.

But there's an even worse problem embedded in the retirement calculation. Retirement calculators almost all make the same erroneous assumption—that our return is the same each and every year. For example, in the calculation above we assumed that we shall receive a 4% return every year. We already know that in the real world, investment returns are not the same each year. It turns out that the *order* of the good and bad years matters a great deal.

To illustrate this phenomenon I went back to good old Uncle Fred's coin toss, with its return of either −10% or +30%. If over 30 years you toss 15 heads and 15 tails, you earn a compounded rate of 8.17%. If you start with a $1,000,000 portfolio and roll alternating heads and tails over the 30-year period, then you indeed can withdraw $81,700 annually (8.17% of the initial amount) over the next 30 years and still keep the $1,000,000 principal intact. However, if you are unlucky enough to roll 15 straight tails before rolling 15 straight heads, you can withdraw only $18,600 per year before all the money runs out. Reverse the process and roll the 15 heads followed by 15 tails, and you can withdraw $248,600 per year. If you are in the saving phase of an investment program, you are much better off having the bad years at the beginning of your savings program than at the end. In other words, as we've already discussed, younger investors should pray for a bear market, and older investors for a bull market.

This phenomenon was first brought to the attention of the investing public by Philip L. Cooley, Carl M. Hubbard, and Daniel T. Walz from Trinity University. They looked at the "success rate" of various withdrawal strategies over numerous historical periods, and they came to the conclusion that only a withdrawal rate of 4% to 5% of the initial portfolio value (i.e., $40,000–$50,000 of a $1,000,000 portfolio) had a reasonable expectation of success (which they defined as dying without debt). And remember, they were looking at historical data, with 7% real equity returns.

On a more basic level, however, you can apply a much simpler acid test to your withdrawal strategy: What would happen if the day you retired marked the beginning of a long, brutal bear market, say, on January 1, 1966, and you lived for another 30 years, until December 31, 1995? For the first 17 years (1966 to 1982), the return of the S&P 500 was a paltry 6.81%. By gruesome numerical coincidence, this was identical to the rate of inflation for the period, making the real stock return for the whole 1966–1982 period zero. The return for the next 13 years (1983–1995) was spectacular, bringing the real return for the whole 30-year 1966–1995 period up to 5.4%, not too far below the historical norm of 7%.

I constructed an all-equity allocation consisting of 80% S&P 500 and 20% U.S. small stocks, and mixed this with five-year Treasuries. I assumed that one began the period with $1,000,000 and then calculated results of various withdrawal rates from the following mixes: 100% stock, 100% bond, and 75/25, 50/50, and 25/75 mixes of both. The results of 7%, 6%, 5%, and 4% withdrawal rates (that is, annually withdrawing $70,000, $60,000, $50,000, and $40,000) are plotted in Figures 8-1 through 8-4. The all-stock portfolio is the thickest line, and the thinner the line, the less stock. Again, it is important to realize that the amounts on the *y* axes are in *inflation-adjusted* 1966 dollars. This is the simplest and clearest way of performing this sort of calculation.

The results are profoundly disturbing. Since real equity returns were over 5.5% during this period, this means that a "penalty" of about 1%–2% was extracted by "the luck of the draw." This means that if future real portfolio returns are going to be only 4%, then in a *worst case* scenario you may only be able to withdraw 2% of the starting amount of your nest egg each year. And this gets to the heart of how we perceive risk. The odds are that you will not encounter the worst case of a prolonged and profound bear market at the beginning of your retirement. In fact, it is equally likely that the opposite may occur—a prolonged bull market at the beginning— and that you will be sitting in unexpected clover, able to withdraw 6% or more of your starting amount each year. But we cannot

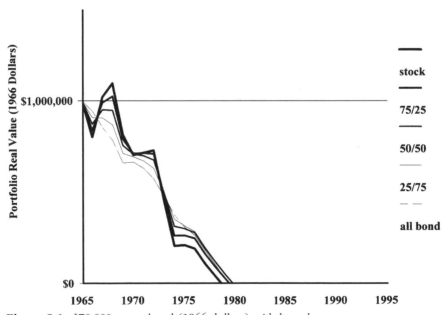

Figure 8-1. $70,000 annual real (1966 dollars) withdrawal.

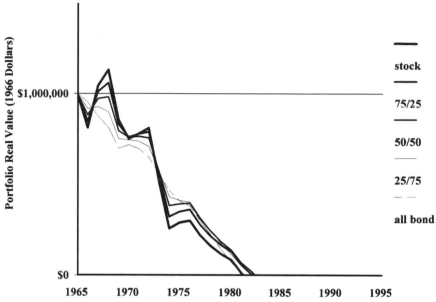

Figure 8-2. $60,000 annual real (1966 dollars) withdrawal.

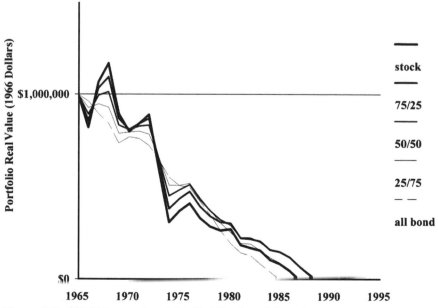

Figure 8-3. $50,000 annual real (1966 dollars) withdrawal.

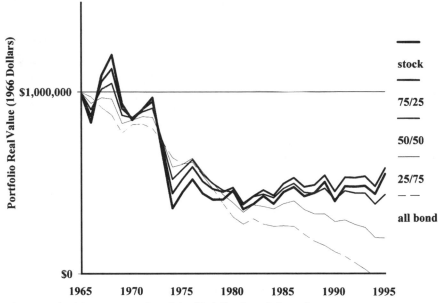

Figure 8-4. $40,000 annual real (1966 dollars) withdrawal.

forecast the future. If you plan "reasonable" withdrawals, there is only a small risk of disaster, which you can lessen by lowering your retirement living standards.

Finally, Uncle Sam has provided a tempting way out of this dilemma—Treasury Inflation-Protected Securities (TIPS) currently yield a 4% inflation-adjusted return. If you can live on 4% of before-tax savings, *and* you can shelter almost all of your retirement money in a Roth IRA (which would not require mandatory distributions after age 70^1/$_2$), then you are guaranteed success for up to 30 years. For devout believers in the value of a well-diversified portfolio, this option is profoundly disturbing—the financial equivalent of Eden's snake. I find it hard to recommend this path. However, at a minimum a healthy commitment to TIPS in your tax-sheltered account is probably not a bad idea.

Cousin Harry Asks Your Advice

Decades pass; you have all but taken over the family business from Uncle Fred, whose duties have become increasingly ceremonial.

Your beloved uncle retains one important area of control: the retirement fund.

Your younger cousin Harry is a fairly recent hire. One day he walks into your office with a quizzical look on his face. Even before he opens his mouth, you know why he has come: Uncle Fred has just made him an offer. By now you have gained a reputation about matters financial equal to that of your uncle, but unlike him you are not given to Socratic teaching. You are very busy, so you try to answer questions as directly as possible. What advice can you give Cousin Harry?

1. *Risk and reward are inextricably entwined.* Do not expect high returns from safe assets; investments with historically high returns are capable of inflicting ferocious losses.

2. *Those who do not learn from history are condemned to repeat it.* Become familiar with the long-term history of the behavior of different classes of stocks and bonds; the surprised investor is a failed investor.

3. *Portfolios behave differently than their constituent parts.* A safe portfolio does not necessarily exclude very risky assets; excessive reliance on safe assets may actually increase portfolio risk. Even the investor who seeks the safest possible portfolio will own some risky assets; a portfolio consisting of "safe" large stocks will often have less return and higher risk than one partitioned between risky smaller stocks and cash.

4. *For a given degree of risk, there is a portfolio that will deliver the most return; this portfolio occupies the efficient frontier of portfolio compositions.* The investor obviously seeks a portfolio that sits on the efficient frontier; unfortunately, its location becomes known only in retrospect. The investor's objective, then, is not to find the efficient frontier; that is impossible. Rather, the goal of the intelligent asset allocator is to find a portfolio mix that will come reasonably close to the mark under a broad range of circumstances. Portfolios consisting of a wide variety of domestic and foreign large and small stocks, and whose bonds are both foreign and domestic, seem to do this the best.

5. *Focus on the behavior of your portfolio, not on its constituent parts.* Small portions of your portfolio will often sustain serious losses, but will cause only minor damage to the whole portfolio.

6. *Recognize the benefits of rebalancing.* The correct response to a fall in asset price is to buy a bit more; the correct response to a rising price is to lighten up a bit. Rebalancing is merely a disciplined way of accomplishing this. Prolonged market declines will make rebalancing seem a frustrating waste of money; in the end, however, asset prices almost always turn around, and you usually will be rewarded handsomely for your patience.

7. *The markets are smarter than you are; they are also smarter than the experts.* Remember that a stopped clock is right twice a day. Even the most inept analyst occasionally makes a good call, and he will probably be interviewed by Lou Rukeyser soon after he has made it. Nobody consistently predicts market direction. Very few money managers beat the market in the long run; those that have done so in the recent past are unlikely to do so in the future. Do not run with the crowd; those who follow the elephant herd often get dirty and squashed.

8. *Know how expensive the tomatoes are.* Keep an eye on market valuation. Changes in your policy allocation should be made only in response to valuation changes, and they should be made in a direction opposite to the price of the asset. Remember that market history teaches us that economic and political considerations are worthless as market predictors; the best times to buy are when things seem the bleakest.

9. *Good companies are usually bad stocks; bad companies are usually good stocks.* Favor a "value" approach in your stock and mutual fund choices; the P/B ratio is the best indicator of this.

10. *In the long run, it is very hard to beat a low-expense index mutual fund.* Try to index as many of your investments as you can; bond fund expenses should be less than 0.5%, domestic stock fund expenses less than 0.7%, and foreign fund expenses less than 1%.

9

Investment Resources

If you're like me, you forget much of what you have read after a relatively brief period of time. If you are managing even a modest asset pool, the material covered herein is simply too important to forget. No, I'm not suggesting that you periodically reread this book. Rather, I suggest that you make finance part of your regular reading program. If you read just one useful book on finance per year, you will wind up better informed than most professionals, and your fiscal health will improve as well. All of the books I shall recommend are quite well written and should not serve as substitutes for sleeping medicine.

A Modest Reading List

1. *A Random Walk Down Wall Street,* by Burton Malkiel. An excellent investment primer, it explains the basics of stocks, bonds, and mutual funds and will reinforce the efficient-market concept.

2. *Common Sense on Mutual Funds.* Replaces *Bogle on Mutual Funds,* by who else, John Bogle. This will provide more detail than you ever wanted to know about this important investment vehicle. Mr. Bogle is the chairman and founder of the Vanguard Group, and he has been an important voice in the industry for decades. Beautifully written, opinionated, and highly recommended. The book also demonstrates the democratization which has swept the investment industry in recent years. Until a decade ago, the sort of sophisticated mutual fund analysis described in his book was the brief of just a handful of professionals with access to expensive

proprietary databases and mainframe computers. Almost all of Bogle's work was done with a subscription to Morningstar and a statistically competent assistant; it could have been performed by any small investor with similar software and ability.

3. *Asset Allocation*, by Roger Gibson. This covers much of the same ground as this book, with more emphasis on the qualities of individual assets. Oriented toward the financial advisor.

4. *Global Investing*, by Roger Ibbotson and Gary Brinson. This is a beautifully written volume on the history of investible assets. An informed investor cannot know enough about market history, and this is the best single source in this area. Want to know what the returns for U.S. stocks have been in each of the past 200 years? The price of gold for the past 500 years? Interest rates and inflation for the past 800 years? It's all here. As implied by the title, the authors also provide an excellent perspective on the place of foreign assets in a diversified portfolio. They provide some worthwhile insights on portfolio theory and the efficiency of the marketplace.

5. *What Has Worked in Investing* is a free pamphlet from Tweedy, Browne. A low-key sales pitch for their funds, it is also the best compilation I've seen of the data supporting the value method. The phone number is 1-800-873-8242. It is also available online at http://www.tweedy.com.

6. *The New Finance: The Case Against Efficient Markets*, by Robert Haugen. If you're intrigued by the Tweedy pamphlet and wonder why value investing still works after all these years, this is your book. The prose is breezy, even quirky—Ben Graham meets Hunter Thompson on bad acid.

7. *Value Averaging*, by Michael Edleson. An extremely useful how-to book on deploying a lump sum of money among multiple assets. Unfortunately out of print, with luck it can be found on the shelf of a large secondhand bookstore.

8. *The Intelligent Investor*, by Ben Graham. A popularized and more readable version of his earlier classic, *Security Analysis*, written with David Dodd. Although it has great relevance to the markets in general and should be read by any serious investor, it is particularly pertinent to anybody who feels compelled to buy individual stocks. Many of today's most successful money managers obtained their

original financial inspiration from these two books. It is always fun to look at excesses in the marketplace and ask, "What would Ben say about this?" (By the way, if you get bitten by the Graham bug and decide to read *Security Analysis*, make sure you read the original 1934 edition, recently reprinted by McGraw-Hill.)

9. *The Wall Street Journal.* The WSJ is actually three newspapers. The first section is a superb national newspaper with incisive commentary on the major issues facing modern society, as well as a surprising dollop of whimsy. First-time readers will also be surprised at the liberal bent of many of the articles. The second section is a marketing periodical, and makes excellent fish wrap. The third section contains the most complete financial data available in a daily paper, as well as financial commentary. Once a week a section on personal finance appears, "Getting Going," covering personal investing, individual assets, tax and retirement strategy, and even some portfolio theory. This series alone is worth the subscription price. I have a file of these articles at home that is constantly growing.

10. Join the American Association of Individual Investors. The fee for this is nominal, and with membership you get the *AAII Journal*, which contains many excellent articles on personal finance.

11. If you have a PC at home or at work, subscribe to Morningstar's mutual fund database. This costs from $95 to over $600 per year, depending on update frequency and depth of data; it is simply the best bargain in investing. The service is an effective way to deal with the more than 10,000 mutual funds currently available. The major advantage of this software is that it allows you to customize your criteria for fund selection. If you are not computer-literate, Morningstar has a print listing of mutual funds using the Value Line format; it costs about $300 per year and is available at most large public libraries.

For those few readers who were intrigued by the mathematical and theoretical aspects of this book, I would also recommend the following:

12. *Portfolio Selection*, by Harry Markowitz. Describes in fairly understandable terms mean-variance analysis. The more formal text, *Mean-Variance Analysis in Portfolio Choice and Capital Markets*, is inaccessible to all but those with extensive mathematical back-

grounds. I found it remarkable that most of the analysts I have spoken to have not read either book.

13. *Stocks, Bonds, Bills, and Inflation*, from Ibbotson Associates. Contains extremely detailed financial data on many important U.S. assets going back to 1926, as well as an excellent description of the mathematical operations involved in asset and portfolio analysis.

Finally, I'm often asked how I "keep up" with finance. Actually, a more accurate term would be "keep back." The most effective way of coping with current market conditions is to learn as much about market history as you possibly can. A superb place to start is Charles Mackay's *Memoirs of Extraordinary Popular Delusions and the Madness of Crowds*, originally published in 1841, and easily available from reprinted editions. The first chapters detail the Mississippi Scheme, South Sea Bubble, and Tulipomania of centuries ago. Change a few of the names and you're reading about Internet stocks.

Also, I suggest almost anything by James Grant, whose entertaining prose and grasp of financial history are second to none. (*Money of the Mind, Minding Mr. Market*, and *The Trouble with Prosperity* are all excellent places to start.)

If you *really* want to keep up, subscribe to the *Journal of Finance* ($80 per year, along with membership in the American Finance Association) and *Financial Analysts Journal* (about $150 per year). The pieces tend to be abstruse, jargonistic, and strewn with incomprehensible formulae, but about once per issue there is a truly important and comprehensible piece which pays for the subscription. For hard-core finance types only.

Useful Websites for the Asset Allocator

When I wrote the previous versions of this book, I was not impressed with the quality of advice and data available on-line. No longer—there is now a cornucopia of useful information out there. Below is a very incomplete list:

Investing for the 21st Century (http://www.fee-only-advisor.com/ book/index.html): Frank Armstrong's grandaddy of all on-line investing books. Frank's perspective is similar to my own, except that he's funnier and better looking. His dog, Schatzke, is better at market timing than anyone else on Wall Street. Chapter 22 in particular is a classic send-up of *Wall Street Week.*

InvestorHome (http://www.investorhome.com): A collection of investment data and media links.

FINWEB (http://www.finweb.com): Academic finance's superb web resource locator.

Research Journals in Finance (http://www.cob.ohio-state.edu/dept/fin/resources_research/rsjnl.htm): Links to a growing list of on-line academic journals.

TAM Asset Management (http://www.tamasset.com): Jeff Troutner's asset-class-based website. Publishes *Asset Class*, a periodic review of asset behavior. Jeff also posts annual returns of many of the DFA/MSCI/Ibbotson data series at the following Web address: http://www.tamasset.com/allocation.html.

Barra (http://www.barra.com) and Wilshire (http://www.wilshire.com): Both sites offer superb asset-class data downloads. Barra is probably the best way of following market valuation, with a unique historical compilation of U.S. valuation measures, while Wilshire has more extensive monthly returns data.

Global Financial Data (http://www.globalfindata.com): Brian Taylor's data service, provides a panoramic view of global asset returns over time and space.

Morgan Stanley Capital Indexes (http://www.mscidata.com): Downloadable returns for all of the MSCI national and regional indexes. (These are available as monthly index values. To obtain the monthly index return, download the "gross return" indexes and then divide that month's return index by the previous month's return index.)

Bloomberg (http://www.bloomberg.com): Probably the best way to keep up with the global marketplace, minute by minute.

Financial Engines (http://www.financialengines.com): Nobelist Bill Sharpe's asset allocation service. You can see the future, but does it work? Also see his excellent homepage.

Journal of Finance (http://www.afajof.org): If it's important, it's likely to be published here first. Unfortunately, it's not always in plain English.

Mutual fund companies: Almost every fund family has a nearly worthless promotional site, and in general I'd stay away. There are three delightful exceptions: Vanguard (http://www.vanguard.com) has a full-service site with downloadable prospectuses/applications/annual reports, on-line account servicing, and a great deal of asset-class-based educational materials, DFA's site (http://www.dfafunds.com) is also worth visiting, even if it is a bit difficult to navigate around. Finally, the Tweedy's Browne site (http://www.tweedy.com) features their pamphlets, especially *What Has Worked in Investing*. Their annual reports are well worth reading.

Appendix A

Becoming Your Own Portfolio Analyst

This section is for those very few readers who are interested in the details of the spreadsheet analyses and mean-variance optimizers referred to in this book. You will need some familiarity with spreadsheet writing, particularly the "copy" commands that enable you to seed a given formula into large cell blocks.

I've posted a compressed template Excel spreadsheet that calculates the annualized returns and SDs for the 1970–1998 period at: http://www.efficientfrontier.com/files/sample.exe.

The returns data are fictitious: I would have liked to place the actual data in it, but unfortunately these are copyrighted. You will have to obtain it on your own. Fortunately, a fair amount of monthly and annual returns series are now available on the Internet. See the TAM Asset Management, MSCI, Wilshire, and Barra sites mentioned in Chapter 9 for more information. The Ibbotson data is available relatively inexpensively from its annual yearbook, *Stocks, Bonds, Bills, and Inflation*. The best single-page listing of asset-class returns is on Jeff Troutner's TAM Asset Management site (http://www.tamasset.com.allocation.html), where he posts annual returns from 1973 for the major U.S. and foreign style-based indexes and intermediate Treasuries.

Mean-Variance Optimizers

Until recently, mean-variance optimizers were overpriced (most still are) and simply not cost-effective if you had a spreadsheet optimizer set up. Fortunately, I was able to convince a colleague, David Wilkinson, to write and market a pair of inexpensive optimizers (VisualMVO and

MVOPlus), starting at $99, and available from Efficient Software (http://www.effisols.com). He may never forgive me.

Be aware that you are entering a sensitive area for most financial professionals. Most "retail" investment professionals such as mutual fund salespeople and brokerage "account executives" are at best only dimly aware of portfolio theory and MVO. Those that are familiar with these areas form the elite of the investment business, and tend to be managers of large investment pools. These folks treat portfolio theory a little like the trade secrets of a medieval guild; don't expect a lot of help from them.

So you're on your own. As discussed in Chapter 5, mean-variance analysis is *not* terribly useful for the design of your portfolio. Rather, it is primarily a teaching tool that you will find helpful for learning about portfolio behavior. At most it is sometimes useful in answering certain highly specific questions. For example, suppose you are wondering about the role of, say, precious metals equity (PME) in your allocation. You would then set up a simple MVO analysis consisting of three assets: the stock and bond portions of your portfolio and PME. You might then adjust the return of PME up or down in order to determine the returns required for its inclusion in a portfolio. (Of course, you will need to have a good idea of its SD and correlation with the rest of the portfolio in order to do this.) If your analysis shows that precious metals equity starts appearing in your portfolio at a return of, say, 5%, then it might be reasonable to use it. On the other hand, if your analysis shows that a return of 10% is required, you might be wary, as the long-term return of precious metals equity is likely not that high.

Appendix B

Correlation Coefficients Among Asset Classes

The following are the correlation matrixes for three different time periods. The values listed below will vary somewhat with the period sampled as well as with the interval measured; for example, the correlation coefficient for large and small U.S. stock returns from 1926 through 1998 is different for monthly, quarterly, and annual periods.

For the 1926–1998 Ibbotson data, the correlations for annual returns are as listed in Table B-1, the correlations for the 1973–1998 database are listed in Table B-2, and the correlations for recent quarterly returns for a somewhat wider range of assets are listed in Table B-3.

Note that small negative correlations are often seen between short-term bonds and many stock assets because rising interest rates usually have a deleterious effect on stock prices while increasing the short-term bond return. The opposite occurs with falling interest rates. This negative correlation is not seen with long-term bonds because the effect of changing interest rates on bond price overwhelms the change in the yield; thus rising rates produces a fall in the total return of both stocks and long bonds. This small but fairly consistent negative correlation between short-term bonds and stocks is the reason why short-term bonds are favored over long-term bonds by many portfolio analysts.

As noted above, correlation coefficients vary somewhat by sampling interval and period; the values in the tables below should be used only as starting points. For example, the correlation of quarterly returns for the 1994–1998 period are in general lower than for monthly or annual returns during the same period.

Table B-1. Correlation Of Annual Returns 1926–1998

	Large U.S. stocks	Small U.S. stocks	20-year Treasuries	5-year Treasuries	30-day Treasuries
Large U.S. stocks	1.00				
Small U.S. stocks	0.79	1.00			
20-year Treasuries	0.20	0.01	1.00		
5-year Treasuries	0.11	−0.05	0.90	1.00	
30-day Treasuries	−0.03	−0.13	0.25	0.50	1.00

Table B-2. Correlation of Annual Returns, 1973–1998

	S&P	USSM	EAFE	HY	LTGC	IB	T-Bill	Gold	NATR	REIT	1 Y	UKSM	JPSM
S&P	1.00												
USSM	0.66	1.00											
EAFE	0.46	0.34	1.00										
HY	0.53	0.57	0.31	1.00									
LTGC	0.57	0.31	0.19	0.65	1.00								
IB	0.06	0.00	0.54	0.26	0.26	1.00							
T-Bill	-0.09	-0.01	-0.15	-0.11	0.06	-0.31	1.00						
Gold	0.09	0.21	0.23	-0.02	-0.06	0.06	0.22	1.00					
NATR	0.53	0.59	0.35	0.13	-0.08	-0.08	0.04	0.56	1.00				
REIT	0.56	0.84	0.33	0.64	0.29	0.01	0.02	0.34	0.62	1.00			
1 Y	-0.04	0.05	-0.11	0.16	0.30	-0.15	0.93	0.15	-0.08	0.08	1.00		
UKSM	0.24	0.41	0.64	0.23	-0.02	0.57	-0.14	0.30	0.34	0.38	-0.13	1.00	
JPSM	0.04	0.06	0.69	0.01	-0.10	0.54	-0.06	0.11	0.16	0.03	-0.10	0.41	1.00

S&P = Standard & Poor's 500, USSM = U.S. Small Stocks (CRSP 9-10 Decile), EAFE = MSCI Europe, Australasia and Far East, HY = First Boston High Yield Bond Index, LTGC = Lehman Bros. Long-Term Government Corporate Bond Index, IB = Salomon Brothers Non-Dollar World Government Bond Index, T-Bill = 30-Day U.S. Treasury Bill, Gold = Morningstar Precious Metals Fund Average, NATR = Morningstar Natural Resources Fund Average, REIT = National Association of Real Estate Investment Trusts (Equity REIT only) Index, 1 Y = One-Year Corporate Bond Index (Dimensional Fund Advisors), UKSM = Hoare-Govett/DFA United Kingdom Small Company Fund, JPSM = Nomura DFA Japan Small Company Fund.

Table B-3. Correlation of Quarterly Returns, 1994–1998

	S&P	USSM	REIT	EAFE	INTSM	EM	EMSM	T-Bond	1 Y	T-Bill	IB	HY	NATR	Gold
S&P	1.00													
USSM	0.77	1.00												
REIT	0.38	0.50	1.00											
EAFE	0.82	0.66	0.09	1.00										
INTSM	0.49	0.51	−0.09	0.84	1.00									
EM	0.69	0.59	0.16	0.69	0.63	1.00								
EMSM	0.57	0.53	0.15	0.57	0.51	0.94	1.00							
T-Bond	0.09	−0.07	0.23	−0.30	−0.54	−0.33	−0.42	1.00						
1 Y	0.47	0.27	0.34	−0.01	−0.23	0.11	0.01	0.71	1.00					
T-Bill	0.18	0.04	0.44	−0.28	−0.45	−0.13	−0.17	0.71	0.74	1.00				
IB	0.35	0.23	−0.03	0.26	0.14	0.11	0.04	0.31	0.51	−0.03	1.00			
HY	0.76	0.76	0.72	0.44	0.19	0.42	0.37	0.26	0.61	0.43	0.36	1.00		
NATR	0.43	0.73	0.67	0.35	0.34	0.45	0.40	−0.12	0.24	0.11	0.16	0.64	1.00	
Gold	0.07	0.31	0.02	0.12	0.37	0.46	0.44	−0.26	0.13	−0.03	0.00	0.08	0.56	1.00

S&P = Standard & Poor's 500, USSM = U.S. Small Stocks (CRSP 9–10 Decile), REIT = National Association of Real Estate Investment Trusts (Equity REIT only) Index, EAFE = MSCI Europe, Australasia, and Far East, INTSM = DFA International Small Company Strategy/Fund, EM = DFA Emerging Markets Fund, EMSM = DFA Emerging Markets Small Company Index/Fund, T-Bond = 20-Year U.S. Treasury Bond Index (Ibbotson Assoc.), 1 Y = One-Year Corporate Bond Index (DFA), T-Bill = 30-Day U.S. Treasury Bill, IB = Salomon Brothers Non-Dollar World Government Bond Index, HY = First Boston High Yield Bond Index, NATR = Morningstar Natural Resources Fund Average, Gold = Morningstar Precious Metals Fund Average.

Glossary

Active management: The process of using security analysis in an attempt to obtain returns higher than those offered by the market.

Alpha: The degree to which a manager's or fund's return differs from that of a benchmark. The benchmark is usually defined in terms of **regression analysis.** For example, an alpha of +0.2% per month means that the manager or fund has exceeded the regression-defined benchmark return by that amount over the period studied. By definition, the market has an alpha of zero.

American depositary receipts (ADRs): Shares issued by a U.S. depositary bank of a foreign company. One ADR share may represent any fixed number of the company's shares trading on its own exchange; i.e., one ADR may represent 2, 10, or 4.5 shares of the stock trading on its domestic bourse. The ADR price is kept at a level nearly identical to the currency-adjusted foreign market price by arbitrage.

Annualized return: The constant return necessary to produce a given return or loss. For example, if a stock returns 0%, 0%, and 33.1% in three successive years, then the annualized return is 10% $(1.1 \times 1.1 \times 1.1 = 1.331)$.

Arbitrage: The simultaneous buying and selling of a given security in different markets at different prices, yielding a riskless profit. (The most prevalent variety is *index arbitrage,* which typically exploits small differences in prices between futures contracts and the underlying stocks.)

Ask price: A broker's price to sell a stock or bond; also called the offer price.

Asset allocation: The process of dividing up one's securities among broad asset classes, i.e., foreign and domestic stocks and foreign and domestic bonds.

Asset class: Categories of stocks, bonds, and other financial assets.

Autocorrelation: The degree to which a given return in a series predicts the next. Like a **correlation,** its value ranges between +1 (where an above or below average return is always followed by an identical return) and −1 (where an above or below average return is always followed by a similar below or above average return). Positive autocorrelations indicate *momentum,* and negative autocorrelations *regression to the mean.* A zero autocorrelation defines a **random walk,** where any given return contains no information about the succeeding return.

Average return: The simple arithmetic average of a series of returns. In the above example of a stock with returns of 0%, 0%, and 33.1% in three successive years, the average return is 11.033%. The average return is of little use to the typical investor—it is almost always larger than the annualized return and often grossly over-estimates the actual return received on the asset.

Beta: The amount which a stock or stock fund tends to move up or down with the market. For example, a beta of 1.3 means that a 1% rise or fall in the market on average results in a 1.3% rise or fall in the security or fund in question. High-beta stocks and funds are risky. A low-beta stock or fund may be less risky, but it may also be highly risky with a low **correlation** with the market. See **capital asset pricing model.**

Bid price: A broker's price to buy a stock or bond.

Bond: Debt issued by a corporation or governmental entity. Carries a **coupon,** or the amount of interest it yields. Bonds are usually of greater than one-year maturity. (Treasury securities of 1–10 years' maturity are called *notes.*)

Book value: A company's assets minus intangible assets and liabilities; very roughly speaking, a company's net assets.

Capital asset pricing model (CAPM): A theory relating risk and expected return. Basically, it states that the return of a security or portfolio is equal to the *risk-free rate* plus a *risk premium* defined by its **beta.** This theory contains a large number of unrealistic assumptions and has been shown to be inconsistent with empirical data (i.e., in the real world it turns out that high-beta stocks do not have higher returns than low-beta stocks).

Capital gain: The amount of profit made on the sale of a security or fund. Determines the amount of applicable tax paid.

Cash flow: Earnings before depreciation and other charges.

Closed-end fund: An investment company that trades like any other corporation, usually does not redeem its shares, and only infrequently issues shares. May trade above (premium) or below (discount) its **net asset value (NAV),** in contradistinction to the more familiar **open-end fund,** or mutual fund, which trades each day at its precise NAV and redeems and issues shares at will.

Commission: The fee paid to a broker to execute a trade.

Contrarian: One who buys or sells unpopular or popular asset classes and securities, thus behaving in a manner contrary to popular sentiment or "conventional wisdom."

Correlation: The degree to which two series of numbers (in finance, usually returns) relate to one another. Ranges between $+1$ (an above/below average return for asset A is always associated with an above/below average return on asset B) and -1 (an above/below average return for asset A is always associated with a below/above average return on asset B). A correlation of zero indicates that the returns of assets A and B are unrelated.

Coupon: The regular interest payment made to the bondholders during the life of the bond. A coupon of 6% on a $1000 bond means that $60 interest will be paid, usually as two semiannual $30 payments.

Currency risk/return: The risk and return associated with holding a foreign security caused by fluctuations in the exchange rate.

Cyclical stock: A security that is particularly sensitive to economic conditions, such as an aircraft or paper company (as opposed to a food or drug manufacturer, whose profits and sales are not sensitive to economic conditions).

Discounted dividend model (DDM). A method of estimating the intrinsic value of a company or market by calculating the discounted value of its expected future dividends. The amount by which future dividends are reduced is called the *discount rate*; it typically approximates the risk-adjusted return of the asset.

Diversification: Allocating assets among investments with different risks, returns, and correlations in order to minimize **nonsystematic risk.**

Efficient frontier: All of the possible portfolio combinations which maximize return for every possible level of expected risk or which minimize expected risk for every possible level of expected return. The mathematical technique for calculating these portfolios, called **mean-variance analysis,** was invented by Harry Markowitz.

Efficient market hypothesis: The concept that markets impound information into prices so well that the analysis of publicly available information will not produce excess returns.

Expense ratio: The portion of the assets spent to run a mutual fund, including management and advisory fees, overhead costs, and 12b-1 (distribution and advertising) fees. The expense ratio does *not* include brokerage **commissions, spreads,** or **market impact costs.**

High-yield ("junk") bond: A debt instrument with a Standard & Poor's rating of BB or less. By definition, such bonds have yields higher than less risky *investment grade* bonds.

Index fund: A mutual fund designed to mimic the returns of a given stock market index, such as the S&P 500.

Indexing: The strategy of exactly matching the performance of a given stock index, such as the S&P 500. See also **passive investing strategy.**

Initial public offering (IPO): The initial, or *primary,* public security sale of a corporation. After the IPO, the security thus issued trades in the *secondary market.*

Institutional investors: Large investment organizations, including insurance companies, depositary institutions, pension funds, and philanthropies.

Ladder: A bond portfolio with equal amounts invested in evenly spaced maturities. For example, a five-year ladder would have equal amounts invested in one, two, three, four, and five-year securities. Most commonly involves Treasury securities.

Liquidity: The level of trading activity, which determines the ease of buying and selling and **market impact.** A security is said to be *liquid* when trading activity is high, with swift trade execution at a narrow **spread.** An *illiquid* security has low trading activity, with a high spread and significant market impact.

Load fund: A mutual fund sold with a sales charge of up to 8.5%, a **no-load fund.**

Market capitalization: Also known as *market cap;* the market value of all of a company's stock. Companies are frequently divided into large-, mid-, and small-cap categories. Most stock indexes are **cap-weighted,** meaning that they are represented in the index in proportion to their market capitalization. This means that such indexes are dominated by their largest growth companies.

Market impact: The increase or decrease in price caused by buying or selling a large amount of a security. This adversely affects the returns of institutional portfolios with high **turnover.**

Market portfolio: A portfolio or index consisting of all of the stocks available to investors, held in proportion to their **market capital ization.** It is closely approximated by the Wilshire 5000, Russell 3000, and CRSP-All indexes.

Market return: The return of the **market portfolio.**

Maturity: The date of a bond's principal repayment.

Mean-variance analysis: See **efficient frontier.**

Modern portfolio theory (MPT): The underlying principles of the risk and return trade-off.

Mutual fund: A portfolio of stocks, bonds, or other assets managed by an investment company, usually for small investors. Mutual funds provide investors with easy access to highly diversified market exposure and are regulated by the Investment Company Act of 1940. See also **load fund** and **no-load fund.**

Net asset value (NAV): The value of a fund's investments. A **no-load mutual fund** is available for purchase or redemption at the NAV, usually on a daily basis. A **closed-end fund** trades in the same manner as a stock, sometimes at a substantial discount or premium to the NAV.

No-load mutual fund: A mutual fund sold without a sales or distribution (12b-1) fee.

Nominal return: Actual return, not adjusted for inflation.

Nonsystematic risk: Portfolio or security risk that can be eliminated by diversification. Also known as *diversifiable risk*. After nonsystematic risk has been eliminated, **systematic risk** remains which cannot be eliminated. (The prefixes get confusing. Systematic risk is nondiversifiable, nonsystematic risk is diversifiable.)

Open-end fund: Generally the same meaning as **mutual fund.** An open-end fund creates and redeems new shares on demand at the **net asset value.** See also **closed-end fund.**

Par value: Maturity or face value of a bond, usually 100.

Passive management, portfolio, or strategy: Refers to a security selection process not involving active security analysis. Essentially the same as **indexing,** except that a passively managed portfolio may reject securities based on mechanical trading, financial, or valuation criteria, and does not need to conform to any particular index.

Portfolio: Any collection of securities.

Portfolio theory: The study of the relationship of overall portfolio risk and return as a function of the risk, return, and correlation of its component parts.

Price-book (P/B) ratio: A ratio obtained by dividing a company's **market capitalization** by its **book value.** May also be calculated on a per-share basis. A measure of cheapness or value; low P/B stocks are usually defined as being cheap, value stocks.

Price-earnings (P/E) ratio: A ratio obtained by dividing a company's **market capitalization** by its earnings. Interpreted in the same manner as the **P/B ratio.**

Random walk: A condition of random, unpredictable security prices, in which the return-series **autocorrelation** is zero.

Real interest rate, real return: The interest rate or return of a security in excess of inflation. A security or portfolio with zero real interest rate or return exactly maintains its inflation-adjusted value. A security or portfolio with a *constant real return* of $x\%$ can maintain an $x\%$ withdrawal rate indefinitely without suffering inflation-induced erosion of payout or principal.

Real estate investment trust (REIT): A property or mortgage management company. Required by statute to remit 95% of earnings to shareholders.

Rebalancing: The process of buying and selling portfolio components so as to maintain a target, or "policy" **asset allocation.**

Regression analysis: A mathematical technique, available in most spreadsheet packages, which determines the relationship of multiple series of numbers. In finance, it is commonly employed to calculate the contribution of known market factors to a portfolio's returns, and the **alpha** (return added or subtracted) of an active manager.

Reinvestment risk: The risk that future bond interest will have to be reinvested at a lower interest rate.

Return: The change in the value of a portfolio over a given period, including dividends and other distributions.

Riskless rate: The return earned on a *riskless asset,* usually a 30- or 90-day Treasury bill. This is the base return that all investors can be expected to earn. According to **modern portfolio theory** and the **capital asset pricing model,** return in excess of the **riskless rate** (also known as the *risk premium*) can only be obtained by bearing *market risk.*

Risky asset: Any asset exposed to *market risk.*

R squared (R^2): The square of the correlation coefficient. It defines the amount of a returns series which can be explained by an index or factor. For example, a mutual fund with a .80 R^2 relative to the S&P 500 has 80% of its returns explained by this index.

Security: Almost any piece of paper that can be traded for value, except for insurance policies, fixed annuities, and futures contracts. Most commonly refers to stocks and bonds.

Semivariance: The **variance** of those returns falling below the mean. Since **variance** measures the scatter of returns both above and below the mean, it is increased by very high returns. Since only returns below the mean are a source of risk, semivariance is felt to be a better measure of risk.

Spread: The difference between the **bid** and **ask** price of a security. The amount of spread is a measure of the **liquidity** of the security.

Standard deviation (SD): A statistical measure of the scatter of a series of numbers. The SD of the returns of a security or portfolio is usually a good estimate of its risk.

Survivorship bias: An upward bias in the estimation of aggregate security or investment company returns caused by the disappearance of the worst performing members of the group.

Systematic risk: The risk of the **market portfolio,** which cannot be diversified away.

Total return: Same as the **return** of a security or portfolio— includes price change, dividends, and other distributions.

Treasury inflation-protected security (TIPS): A Treasury bond or note whose **coupon** and principal payment are indexed to inflation. At a given maturity the difference between the standard Treasury yield and TIPS yield represents the market's estimate of inflation over that period.

Turnover: The portion of a portfolio that is traded in a given period of time, usually expressed in percent per year. For example, in a portfolio with an annual turnover of 200%, the average security position is traded twice per year.

Utility function: A mathematical formula that assigns a precise value to any economic outcome, usually based on return and risk. Used to model or describe investor behavior.

Value stock: A security that sells at a discount to its intrinsic value. Value stocks are often identified by low **price-book** and **price-earnings ratios.**

Variance: A measure of the scatter of numbers around their average value; the square root of the variance is the **standard deviation (SD).** Like SD, the variance of a security's or portfolio's returns is a proxy for its *risk,* or *volatility.*

Yield: The percentage of a security's value paid as dividends.

Zero-coupon bond: A bond in which no periodic coupon is paid; principal and reinvested interest are paid *in toto* at maturity.

Bibliography

Preface

Brinson, Gary P., Hood, L. Randolph, and Beebower, Gilbert L., "Determinants of Portfolio Performance." *Financial Analysts Journal,* July/August 1986.

Brinson, Gary P., Singer, Brian D., and Beebower, Gilbert L., "Determinants of Portfolio Performance II: An Update." *Financial Analysts Journal,* May/June 1991.

Chapter 2

Crowther, Samuel, and Raskob, John J., interview, *Ladies Home Journal,* August 1929.

Ibbotson Associates, *Stocks, Bonds, Bills, and Inflation.* Ibbotson Associates, 1999.

Keynes, John Maynard, *The Collected Writings of John Maynard Keynes, Volume XII, Economic Articles and Correspondence: Investment and Editorial.* Cambridge University Press, 1983.

Chapter 4

Jorion, Phillippe, and Goetzmann, W., "Global Stock Returns in the Twentieth Century." *Journal of Finance,* June 1999.

Chapter 5

Erb, Claude B., Harvey, Campbell, and Viskanta, Tadas E., "Forecasting International Equity Correlations." *Financial Analysts Journal,* November/December 1994.

Gibson, Roger C., *Asset Allocation,* 3rd Ed. McGraw-Hill, 2000.

Ibbotson, Roger G., and Brinson, Gary P., *Global Investing.* McGraw-Hill, 1993.

Malkiel, Burton G., "Returns from Investing in Equity Mutual Funds from 1971 to 1991." *Journal of Finance,* June 1995.

Malkiel, Burton G., *A Random Walk Down Wall Street.* W. W. Norton, 1996.

Markowitz, Harry M., *Portfolio Selection,* 2nd Ed. Basil Blackwell 1991.

Markowitz, Harry M., *Mean-Variance in Portfolio Choice and Capital Markets.* McGraw-Hill, 2000.

Chapter 6

Brealy, Richard A., *An Introduction to Risk and Return from Common Stocks.* M.I.T. Press, 1969.

Graham, John R., and Harvey, Campbell R., "Market Timing Ability and Volatility Implied in Investment Newsletters' Asset Allocation Recommendations." *National Bureau of Economic Research Working Paper No. 4890,* 1995.

Chapter 7

Benartzi, Shlomo, and Thaler, Richard H., "Myopic Loss Aversion and the Equity Premium Puzzle" *The Quarterly Journal of Economics,* February 1995.

Clayman, Michelle, "In Search of Excellence: The Investor's Viewpoint." *Financial Analysts Journal,* May/June 1987.

Dreman, David N., and Berry, Michael A., "Overreaction, Underreaction, and the Low P/E Effect." *Financial Analysts Journal,* July/August 1995. (See also *FAJ,* May/June 1995.)

Dreman, David N., *Contrarian Investment Strategy: The Psychology of Stock Market Success.* Random House, 1979.

Fama, Eugene F., and French, Kenneth R., "The Cross-Section of Expected Stock Returns." *Journal of Finance,* June 1992.

Graham, Benjamin, *The Intelligent Investor.* Harper and Row, 1973.

Graham, Benjamin, and Dodd, David, *Security Analysis: Principles and Techniques.* McGraw-Hill 1934. Reprinted 1996.

Haugen, Robert A., *The New Finance: The Case Against Efficient Markets.* Prentice-Hall, 1995.

Lakonishok, Josef, Shleifer, Andrei, and Vishny, Robert W., "Contrarian Investment, Extrapolation, and Risk." *Journal of Finance,* December 1994.

Miller, Paul F., Jr., "Low P/E and Value Investing," in Ellis, Charles D., ed., *Classics II: Another Investor's Anthology.* Business One Irwin, 1991.

Peters, Thomas J., and Waterman, Robert W. Jr., *In Search of Excellence: Lessons from America's Best Companies.* Harper Collins, 1982.

Siegel, Jeremy, *Stocks for the Long Run.* McGraw-Hill, 2000.

Value Line Graphic Supplement 1994 (valuation historical data).

Chapter 8

Bogle, John C., *Bogle on Mutual Funds.* Dell, 1994.

Bogle, John C., *Common Sense on Mutual Funds.* Wiley, 1999.

Cooley, P. L., Hubbard, C. M., and Walz, D. T., "Sustainable Withdrawal Rates from Your Retirement Portfolio." *Financial Counseling and Planning,* 10(1), 39–47.

Edleson, Michael E., *Value Averaging: The Safe and Easy Strategy for Higher Investment Returns.* International Publishing, 1993.

Index

About the Author

William Bernstein, Ph.D, M.D., is a practicing neurologist in Oregon. He launced the Web site *www.efficient frontier.com* in August 1996. Known for his quarterly journal of asset allocation and portfolio theory, *Efficient Frontier,* Dr. Bernstein is also a principal in the money management firm Efficient Frontier Advisors, is a frequent guest columnist for Morningstar, and is often quoted in *The Wall Street Journal.*